by Carolyn Abram

Facebook® For Dummies®, Portable Edition

Published by
John Wiley & Sons, Inc.
111 River Street
Hoboken, NJ 07030-5774

www.wiley.com

Published by John Wiley & Sons, Inc., Hoboken, New Jersey

Published simultaneously in Canada

For general information on our other products and services, please contact our Customer Care Department within the U.S. at 877-762-2974, outside the U.S. at 317-572-3993, or fax 317-572-4002. For technical support, please visit www.wiley.com/techsupport.

Wiley publishes in a variety of print and electronic formats and by print-on-demand. Some material included with standard print versions of this book may not be included in e-books or in print-on-demand. If this book refers to media such as a CD or DVD that is not included in the version you purchased, you may download this material at http://booksupport.wiley.com. For more information about Wiley products, visit www.wiley.com.

ISBN 978-1-118-31438-8 (pbk); ISBN 978-1-118-33421-8 (e-PDF); ISBN 978-1-118-33211-5 (e-pub)

Manufactured in the United States of America

10 9 8 7 6 5 4 3

Table of Contents

Introduction

Facebook connects you with the people you know and care about. It enables you to communicate, stay up-to-date, and keep in touch with friends and family anywhere. It facilitates your relationships online to help enhance them in person. Specifically, Facebook connects you with the *people* you know around *content* that is important to you. Whether you're the type to take photos or look at them, or write about your life, or read about your friends' lives, Facebook is designed to enable you to succeed. Maybe you like to share websites and news, play games, plan events, or promote your business. Whatever you prefer, Facebook has you covered.

Facebook offers you control. Communication and information sharing are powerful only when you can do what you want within your comfort zone. Nearly every piece of information and means of connecting on Facebook comes with full privacy controls, allowing you to share and communicate exactly how — and with whom — you desire.

Facebook welcomes everyone: students and professionals; grandchildren (as long as they're at least age 13), parents, and grandparents; busy people; socialites; celebrities; distant friends; and roommates. No matter who you are, using Facebook can add value to your life.

About This Book

Here are some of the things you can do with this book:

- **Find out how to represent yourself online.** Facebook lets you create a profile (called a Timeline) that you can share with friends, co-workers, and the people you have yet to meet.

- **Connect and share with people you know.** Whether you're seeking close friends or long-lost ones, family members, business contacts, teammates, businesses, or celebrities, Facebook keeps you connected. Never say, "Goodbye" again . . . unless you want to.
- **Discover how the online tools of Facebook can help enhance your relationships offline.** Photo sharing, event planning, and messaging tools all enable you to maintain an active social life in the real world.
- **Bring your connections off Facebook and on to the rest of the web.** Many websites, games, apps, and services on the Internet can work with your Facebook information to deliver you a better experience.
- **Promote a business, cause, or yourself to the people who can bring you success.** Engaging with people on Facebook can help ensure that your message is heard.

Foolish Assumptions

In this book, I make the following assumptions:

- You're at least 13 years of age.
- You have some access to the Internet, an e-mail address, and a web browser that is not Internet Explorer 6 (Internet Explorer 7, Safari, Chrome, Firefox, and so on are all good).

Conventions Used in This Book

Facebook pages and features — such as the Facebook Groups or the Settings page — are called out with capital letters. Brackets like <*this*> denote generic text that will be different on your screen, such as looking at <*Your Name*>.

I often state my opinions throughout this book. Although I have worked for Facebook in the past, the opinions expressed here represent only my perspective, not that of Facebook. I'm an avid Facebook user and became one long before I worked for Facebook.

Don't forget about the Table of Contents and the Index; you can use these sections to quickly find the information you need.

Icons Used in This Book

What's a *For Dummies* book without icons pointing you in the direction of great information that's sure to help you along your way? In this section, I briefly describe each icon I use in this book.

The Tip icon points out helpful information that is likely to improve your experience.

The Remember icon marks an interesting and useful fact — something that you may want to use later.

The Warning icon highlights lurking danger. With this icon, I'm telling you to pay attention and proceed with caution.

Where to Go from Here

Whether you've been using Facebook for years or this is your first time, I recommend you start by reading Chapter 1, which sets the stage for most of what I describe in detail in the rest of this book. After reading the first chapter, you may have a better sense of which topics will be more relevant to you, and you can, therefore, flip right to them. However, I recommend that *everyone* spend some quality time in Chapter 3, which covers privacy on Facebook. Facebook is an online representation of a community, so it's important that each person understands how to operate in that community to ensure a safe, fun, and functional environment for everyone.

It's time to get started: Let one hand flip the pages of this book, the other drive your computer mouse, and let your mind open up to one of the most popular, fun, and useful websites out there.

Chapter 1

The Many Faces of Facebook

In This Chapter

- Discovering Facebook
- Knowing what you can and can't do on Facebook
- Finding out how Facebook is different from other social sites
- Seeing how different people use Facebook . . . differently
- Signing up and getting started
- Creating your Timeline
- Getting confirmed and verified

Think about the people you interacted with throughout the past day. In the morning, you may have gone to get the paper and chatted with the neighbor. You may have asked your kids what time they'd be home and negotiated with your partner about whose turn it is to cook dinner. Perhaps you spent the day at the office, chatting, joking, and (heaven forbid) getting things done with your co-workers. In the midst of it all, you may have sent an e-mail to all the people in your book club, asking them what book should be next, and what date works for the most people. Maybe while you sat on the bus you read the newspaper, or called your mom to wish her a happy birthday, or searched on your phone for a good restaurant to go to for drinks with friends. This is your world, as it revolves around you.

Each of us has our own version of the world, and as we interact with each other, those worlds intertwine, interplay, and interlock. Maybe your best friend from college was the one to introduce you to the book club, and then someone from the book club recommended a good restaurant. This network of people you interact with — your friends, acquaintances, and loved ones — exists online. Facebook is the online representation of the web of connections between people in the real world. Facebook (and other Internet companies) like to call this network the *social graph*.

Now, you may be asking, if this graph or network exists in the real world, why do I need it online, too? Good question. The answer is that having it online facilitates and improves all your social relationships. In other words, Facebook makes your life easier and your friendships better. It can help with practical things like remembering a friend's birthday or coordinating a party. It can also help with more abstract aspects of relationships, such as staying close with family you aren't physically near or talking about your day with friends.

In this chapter, you read an overview of Facebook and then sign on. Getting set up and familiar with Facebook does take a little work. It may feel a little overwhelming at times, but the reward is worth it — I promise.

What Is Facebook, Exactly?

"Yes, Carolyn," you're saying. "I know Facebook is going to help me stay in touch with my friends and communicate with the people in my life, but what *is* it?"

At its most basic, Facebook is a website. You'll find it through a web browser like Safari, Google Chrome, Firefox, or Internet Explorer, the same way you might navigate to a search engine like Google or to an airline's website to book tickets. Figure 1-1 shows the screen you will probably see when you navigate to `www.facebook.com`.

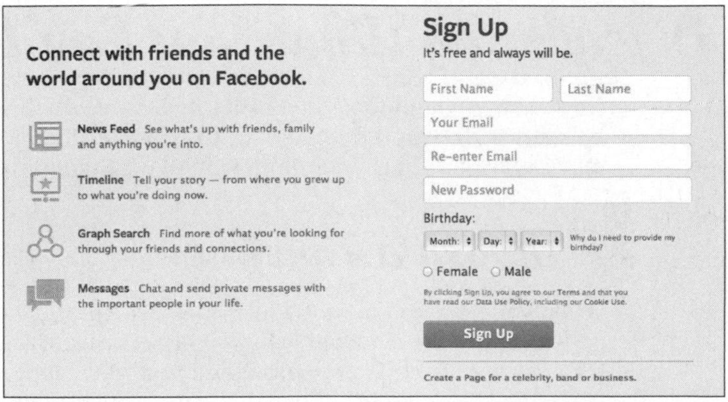

Figure 1-1: Welcome to Facebook. Would you like fries with that?

Facebook is a website where you go to accomplish certain tasks that usually fall under the umbrella category of *social maintenance.* For example, you may go to Facebook to

- Check out what your friends are up to today
- Tell your friends and family about your recent successes, show them your photos, or let them know you're thinking of them
- Show off the pictures from your latest vacation
- Make a contact in a city you're moving to
- Plan an event
- Get in touch with an old friend
- Garner support for a cause
- Get recommendations from friends for movies, books, music, and restaurants
- Remember everyone's birthday

So what Facebook *is,* exactly, is a website built to help you represent yourself online and share with your real-world friends online. The rest of it — how that's accomplished, what people typically share on Facebook, and how it all works — is what this book is all about.

Discovering What You Can Do

Now that you know Facebook is a means by which you can connect with people who matter to you, your next question may be, "How?" In this section, I give you an overview.

Establish a Timeline

When you sign up for Facebook, one of the first things you do is establish your *Timeline,* which will become an ongoing history of your life on Facebook. When you are feeling nostalgic, you can explore your history the same way you might flip through an old photo album.

At first, the thought of putting a photo album of your entire life online may feel scary or daunting. After all, that stuff is personal. But one of the things you'll discover about Facebook is that it's a place to be personal. The people who will see your Timeline are, for the most part, your friends and family members — the people you'd show a photo album to in real life.

That "for the most part" is an important part of Facebook. You will encounter other people on Facebook, including potential employers or professional contacts, more distant friends, and casual acquaintances. Be aware of this distinction — between your close friends and everyone else.

As you start to collect posts, photos, and interactions with friends there, your Timeline becomes an indispensable record of what's going on with you, both now and in the past. The Timeline is set up with all kinds of privacy controls to specify *who* you want to see *which* information. Many people find great value in adding to their Timeline just about every piece of information and then unveiling each particular piece cautiously. The safest rule here is to share on your Timeline only information you'd share with someone in real life.

Chapter 2 provides lots of detail about the Timeline and what you might choose to share there. For now, think of it as a personal web page that Facebook helps you create to facilitate sharing with friends and represent yourself online.

Connect with friends

Now that you know about Timelines, you should also know about ways to connect your Timeline to the Timelines of your acquaintances. These connections are called *friendships.* On Facebook, it's common to refer to *friending* people you know. This just means establishing the virtual connection. Friending people enables you to communicate and share with them more easily. Friends are basically the reason Facebook can be so powerful and useful to people. Facebook offers the following tools to help you find your friends:

- **Facebook Friend Finder:** Enables you to scan the e-mail addresses in your e-mail address book to find whether those people are already on Facebook.
- **People You May Know:** Shows you the names and pictures of people you likely know. These people are selected for you based on commonalities like where you live or work or how many friends you have in common.
- **Search:** Helps you find the people who are most likely already using Facebook.

After you establish a few connections, use those connections to find other people you know by searching through their connections for familiar names. I explain how to find people you know on Facebook in Chapter 4.

Communicate with friends

As Facebook grows, it becomes more likely that anyone with whom you're trying to communicate can be reached. Digging up a person's contact information could require calls to mutual friends, a trip to the white pages, or an e-mail sent to a potentially outdated e-mail address. Facebook streamlines finding and contacting people in one place. If the friend you're reaching out to is active on Facebook, no matter where she lives or how many times she's changed her e-mail address, you can reach one another.

And Facebook isn't just about looking up old friends to say hi. Its messaging system makes it easy to dash a note off to friends and get their reply just as fast. The comments people leave on each other's photos, status updates, and posts are real conversations that you will find yourself taking part in.

Reveal your thoughts

You have something to say. Maybe you're proud of the home team, maybe you're excited about Friday, or maybe you can't believe what you saw on the way to work this morning. All day long, things are happening to all of us that make us just want to turn to our friends and say, "You know what?" Facebook gives you the stage and an eager audience. In Chapter 5, I explain how you can make short or long posts about the things happening around you and how they're distributed to your friends in an easy way.

Share your pictures

Since the invention of the modern-day camera, people have been all too eager to yell, "Cheese!" Photographs can make great tour guides on trips down memory lane, but only if you actually remember to develop, upload, or scrapbook them.

Facebook offers three great incentives for uploading, organizing, and editing your photos:

- **Facebook provides one easy-to-access location for all your photos.** Directing any interested person to your Facebook Timeline is easier than e-mailing pictures individually, sending a complicated link to a photo site, or waiting until the family reunion to show off your pics.
- **Every photo you upload can be linked to the Timelines of the people in the photo.** For example, you upload pictures of you and your sister and link them to her Timeline. Whenever your brother visits her Timeline, he sees those pictures. Photo albums no longer have to be something people look at right after the event and maybe then again years later.

- **Facebook gives you the power to control who has access to your photos.** Every time you upload a photo or create a new photo album on Facebook, you can decide whether you want everyone on Facebook to see it, just your friends, or even a subset of your friends. This control enables you to tailor your audience to those friends who might be most interested. All your friends might enjoy your baby photos, but maybe only your co-workers will care about photos from the company party.

Try out games and apps

In Chapter 8, I explain the games, apps, and websites that you can use with your Facebook information. These websites and applications include tools to help you edit your photos; create slideshows; play games with friends across the globe; divvy up bills among people who live or hang out together; and exchange information about good movies, music, books, and restaurants. After you become a little more comfortable with the Facebook basics, try some of the apps and websites whose services allow you to interact with your Facebook friends.

Knowing What You Can't Do

Facebook is meant to represent real people and real associations; it's also meant to be safe. Many of the rules of participation on Facebook exist to uphold those two goals.

You can't lie

Okay, you can, but you shouldn't, especially not about your basic information. Lying about your identity is a violation of the Statement of Rights and Responsibilities and grounds for disabling your Timeline. Facebook doesn't let anyone sign up with an obviously fake name like Marilyn Manson or Fakey McFakerson. Those who do make it past the name checks will likely find their account flagged and disabled.

You can't be twelve

Or younger. Facebook takes seriously the U.S. law that prohibits minors under the age of 13 from creating an online Timeline for themselves. If you're reported to the Facebook User Operations team and they confirm that you're underage, your account will be disabled.

You can't troll or spam

On the Internet, *trolling* refers to posting deliberately offensive material to websites to get people upset. *Spamming* refers to sending bulk promotional messages. If you do either of these things on Facebook, there's a good chance your account will be shut down. If you're getting warnings about spamming, chances are you just need to tweak *how* you're using Facebook. For example, you may need to create a Page instead of using your personal account for mass messaging.

You can't upload illegal content

Facebook users live in virtually every country in the world, so Facebook is often obligated to respect the local laws, regardless of its own position on pornography (where minors can see it), copyrighted material, hate speech, depictions of crimes, and other offensive content. However, doing so is also in line with Facebook's value of being a safe, happy place for people 13 and older. Don't confuse this with censorship; Facebook is all about freedom of speech and self-expression, but the moment that freedom compromises anyone's safety or breaks any law, disciplinary action is taken.

Realizing How Facebook Differs from Other Social Sites

Lots of social sites besides Facebook try to help people connect. Some popular sites are Twitter, LinkedIn, Google+, Instagram, Tumblr, and many others.

I'll start with the biggest reason Facebook is different. Literally, the biggest: Facebook has over one *billion* users across the world (yes, billion with a *b*). Other social sites might be popular in one country or another, but Facebook is popular pretty much everywhere.

If you're going to use only one social networking site, choose Facebook — everyone you want to interact with is already there.

You'll see a lot of similar functionality across different sites: establishing connections, creating Timelines, liking content, and so on. However, each site brings a slightly different emphasis in terms of what is important. LinkedIn, for example, helps people with career networking, so it puts emphasis on professional information and connections. Match.com, on the other hand, is about matchmaking, so it's not exactly meant for those of us who aren't looking to get a date. Twitter encourages its members to share short *Tweets,* 140-character posts with their connections; and Instagram (which is actually owned by Facebook) encourages its members to share cool photos taken with mobile phones.

You might find some or all of these sites useful at different points in time, but Facebook wants to be the one that is always useful in one way or another — so it tries to offer all the functionality I just mentioned . . . *and more.*

Discovering How You Can Use Facebook

Now that you know what you can do, generally, on Facebook, it's time to consider some of the specific ways you may find yourself using Facebook in the future. The following list is by no means comprehensive, and I've left out some of the things already mentioned in this chapter (things like sharing photos and events). These are more specific-use cases than an advertisement for Facebook's features.

One billion people use Facebook, but not all of them can see your whole Timeline. You can share as much or as little with as many or as few people as you so desire. Put under lock and key the posts or parts of your Timeline you *don't* want to share with everyone. Chapter 3 goes into much greater detail on how to protect yourself and your information.

Getting information

At any age, you may need to find someone's phone number or connect with a friend of a friend to organize something. Facebook can make these very practical tasks a little bit easier. As long as you can search for someone's name, you should be able to find her on Facebook and find the information you're looking for.

Keeping up with long-distance friends

These days, families and friends are often spread far and wide across state or country lines. Children go to college; grandparents move to Florida; people move for their job or because they want a change of scenery. These distances make it hard for people to interact in any more significant way than gathering together once per year to share some turkey and pie (pecan, preferably). Facebook offers a place where you can virtually meet and interact. Upload photos of the kids for everyone to see; write posts about what everyone is up to. Even the more mundane information about your life ("I'm at jury duty") can make someone across the world feel like, just for a second, she's sitting next to you and commiserating with you about your jury summons.

Moving to a new city

Landing in a new city with all your worldly belongings and an upside-down map can be hugely intimidating. Having some open arms or at least numbers to call when you arrive can greatly ease the transition. Although you may already know some people who live in your new city, Facebook can help connect with all the old friends and acquaintances you either forgot live there or have moved there since you last heard from them. These people can help you find doctors, apartments, hair stylists, Frisbee leagues, and restaurants.

As you meet more and more new friends, you can connect with them on Facebook. Sooner than you thought possible, when someone posts about construction slowing down his commute, you know exactly the street he means, and you may realize, *I'm home.*

Getting a job

Plenty of people use Facebook as a tool for managing their careers as well as their social lives. If you're looking at a particular company, find people who already work there to get the inside scoop or to land an interview. If you're thinking about moving into a particular industry, browse your friends by past jobs and interests to find someone to connect with. If you go to a conference for professional development, you can keep track of the other people you meet there as your Facebook friends.

Am I signing up for a dating site?

Throughout this book, you read about ways to communicate: messages, chatting, poking, liking, and commenting. These fairly neutral activities can take on a whole new meaning and spark when they happen between two people interested in each other.

Although Facebook is not technically a dating site, plenty of people do take advantage of its social nature to boost their dating lives in different ways:

- You can inform people through your Timeline whom you're looking to meet (women, men, or both).
- You can certainly use Facebook's systems to flirt, get to know, and yes, do a little background research on dating prospects.
- If you're happily ensconced in couple-dom, listing your relationship status and linking to your partner's Timeline is an easy way to broadcast, "Move along; I'm taken."

Reunions

Thanks to life's curveballs, your friends at any given time may not be the people in your life at another. The memories of people you consider to be most important in your life fade over the years so that even trying to recall a last name may give you pause. The primary reason for this lapse is a legitimate one: There are only so many hours in a day. While we make new, close friends, others drift away because it's impossible to maintain many intense relationships. Facebook is an extremely powerful tool; however, it hasn't yet found a way to extend the number of hours in a day, so it can't exactly fix the problem of growing apart. Facebook can, however, lessen the finality and inevitability of the distance.

Because Facebook is less than ten years old (and because you're reading this book), you probably don't have your entire social history mapped out. Some may find it a daunting task to create connections with everyone they've ever known, which I don't recommend. Instead, build your graph as you need to or as opportunity presents. Perhaps you want to upload a photo taken from your high school graduation. Search for the people in the photo on Facebook; form the friend connection; and then *tag,* or mark, them as being in the photo. Maybe you're thinking about opening a restaurant, and you'd like to contact a friend from college who was headed into the restaurant business after graduation. Perhaps you never told your true feelings to the one who got away. For all these reasons, you may find yourself using the Facebook search box.

Frequently, I receive reports from adopted children who connect with their biological parents or estranged siblings who find each other on Facebook. I once heard from my sixth-grade bully, who found me on Facebook and apologized for his behavior as a kid. I, in turn, used it to apologize to someone I treated terribly around the same time.

Organizing movements

If you kept up on the news of the "Arab Spring" uprisings in the early part of 2011, you couldn't avoid hearing about the role Facebook played. Young people used Facebook as an organizing tool, letting each other know about protest locations and times. People in geographically distant regions could share ideas about their countries and what they wanted to see outside of the watchful eye of oppressive regimes.

And as the drama unfolded, plenty of people with family in the affected areas turned to Facebook to make sure their loved ones were okay. People unrelated but concerned offered their support through their own status updates and more.

The birth of the 'Book

In the old days, say, ten years ago, most college freshmen would receive a thinly bound book containing the names and faces of everyone in their matriculating class. These *face books* were useful for matching names to the students seen around campus or for pointing out particular people to friends. There were several problems with these face books. If someone didn't send in his picture, the books were incomplete. They were outdated by junior year because many people looked drastically different, and the books didn't reflect the students who had transferred in or who were from any other class. Finally, they had little information about each person.

In February 2004, Mark Zuckerberg, a sophomore at Harvard, launched an online "book" to which people could upload their photos and personal information, a service that solved many of these problems. Within a month, more than one-half the Harvard undergraduates had signed up.

Zuckerberg was then joined by others to help expand the site into other schools. I was the first Stanford student to receive an account. During the summer of the same year, Facebook moved to Palo Alto, California, where the site and the company kept growing. By December 2004, the site had grown to one million college students. Every time Facebook opened to a new demographic — high school, then work users, then everyone — the rate at which people joined the site continued to increase.

At the end of 2006, the site had more than 10 million users; 2007 closed out with more than 50 million active users. At the time of this book's publication in 2013, that final count has grown to in excess of one billion people across the globe using Facebook to stay in touch.

The term *movement,* here, can apply to anything. Whether it's a campaign to raise awareness about gay teen suicides or a campaign to raise money for victims of a natural disaster, Facebook can be used to bring support and spread the word.

Signing Up for Facebook

Officially, all you need to join Facebook is a valid e-mail address. When I say *valid,* I just mean that you need to be able to easily access the messages in that account because Facebook e-mails you a registration confirmation. Figure 1-2 shows the crucial part of the sign-up page, which you can find by navigating to `www.facebook.com`.

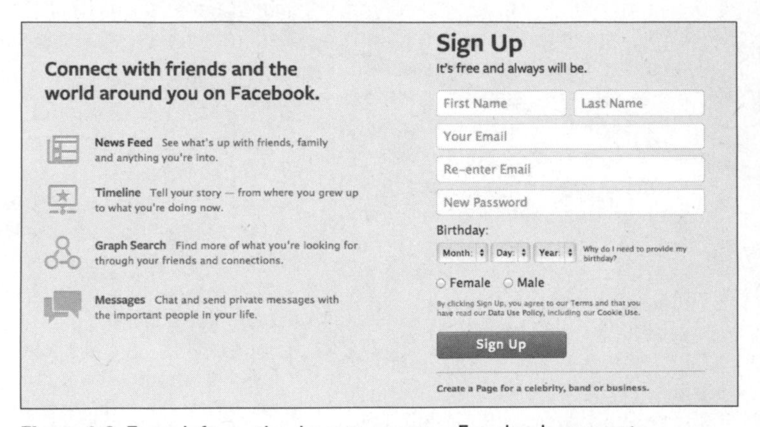

Figure 1-2: Enter information here to create a Facebook account.

As you can see, you need to fill out a few things:

- **First and Last Name:** Facebook is a place based on real identity. Sign up with the name people know you by. I don't recommend signing up with a fake name or alias because that will make it hard for you to be found by friends. After you've signed up, you can add nicknames or maiden names to your Timeline to make it even easier for friends to find you.
- **Email:** You need to enter your valid e-mail address. Facebook asks you to enter your e-mail twice to make sure that there are no typos.

- **Password:** Use a combination of letters and numbers for your password and don't use the same password you use on another site.
- **Birthday:** Enter your date of birth. If you're shy about sharing your birthday, don't worry: You'll be able to hide this information on your Timeline later.
- **Gender (Female or Male):** Facebook uses your gender information to construct sentences about you on the site. If you want to hide your gender on your Timeline, you can do so after you sign up.

After you fill out this information, click Sign Up (that's the big green button). Congratulations: You officially joined Facebook!

When you click Sign Up, you're agreeing to Facebook's Statement of Rights and Responsibilities and Privacy Policy. For details, follow the Terms link.

Getting Started

Facebook puts all its users through a three-step Getting Started Wizard to help start them out on the right foot. In this section, we go through all three of these steps together, covering what to enter as well as why these steps are important to using Facebook.

In certain cases, depending on whether you were invited to join Facebook by a friend or you joined with an e-mail address from your workplace or school, you may get slightly different steps than those detailed as follows. Don't worry; the same principles apply.

Step 1: Find Your Friends

The Find Your Friends step, shown in Figure 1-3, is first because it's that important to enjoying Facebook. Without friends, Facebook can feel a little bit like going to an amusement park alone. Sure, the rides were fun, and the food was greasy, but no one was there to appreciate it with you.

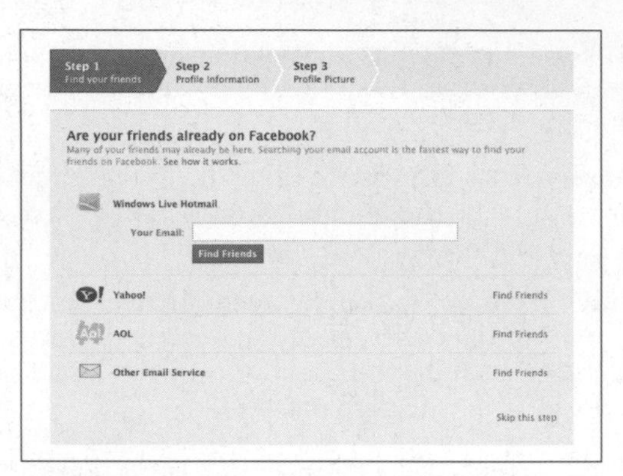

Figure 1-3: Find your friends early and often.

You have many ways to find friends on Facebook. I go over all of them in Chapter 4. The method Facebook is highlighting in this step is the *Friend Finder*.

The Friend Finder works by allowing Facebook access to your e-mail account. Facebook then combs through your e-mail contacts and matches the e-mails it finds with e-mails attached to the Facebook accounts of the people you e-mail. So if Joe Smith, your friend, e-mailed you from `jsmith@email.com` and also had a Facebook account he created with that e-mail address, the Friend Finder presents you with Joe's name and profile picture and asks if you want to be friends on Facebook.

To use the Friend Finder, follow these steps:

1. **Select the e-mail provider you're using.**

   Facebook automatically selects a provider based on the e-mail you used to register. (I used a nonstandard domain, so nothing is prefilled in Figure 1-3.)

   Depending on what e-mail service you use, importing your contacts and looking for friends may entail a few extra steps. Facebook provides instructions for these steps. If you follow those steps, come back here and skip to Step 4 on this list.

2. **Enter your e-mail address and e-mail password.**

   Remember to enter your e-mail password, not the password you just created for Facebook.

3. **Click Find Friends.**

   Behind the scenes, Facebook searches your contact list and presents you with the people in your e-mail Contacts list who are already on Facebook. By default, all these people are selected to be your friends.

4. **Look through the list and choose the people you want to be friends with on Facebook.**

   I talk more about *who,* exactly, should be your Facebook friends in Chapter 4, but for now, a good rule is to look for people you're friends with or related to in real life. You can deselect the people you don't want to add by clicking their faces or the check boxes.

   This isn't your only opportunity to use the Friend Finder. If you aren't sure about adding a lot of people right away, that's okay. Chapter 4 shows you how to get back to these steps at any point in time.

5. **Click Add as Friends.**

   This sends *Friend Requests* to all the people you selected in Step 4. On Facebook, all friendships have to be agreed to by both people. A request to your friend needs to be approved by her before you are officially Facebook friends.

   After you add friends, Facebook looks at the e-mail addresses it didn't find matches for and asks you whether you want to invite those people to join Facebook.

6. **Select people you want to invite to join Facebook.**

   Much like selecting friends to add, you can select and deselect friends' e-mail addresses by selecting the check box next to their e-mails.

   If you don't want to invite anyone to join Facebook just yet, look on the bottom right of the screen for a Skip link. It's right next to the Send Invites button.

7. **Click Send Invites to send out invitations to your friends via e-mail.**

   They'll receive e-mails from Facebook letting them know you invited them to join.

The Friend Finder is useful when you're just getting started on Facebook because it allows you to find a whole bunch of friends all at once. If you had to look for each of your friends by name, it could take a while. Friend Finder allows you to speed up that process.

Step 2: Profile Information

Your *Facebook Profile,* or *Timeline,* is the online representation of who you are. Most likely, you have online profiles for various websites. Facebook Timelines tend to be a little more comprehensive and dynamic, for reasons that I detail in Chapter 2.

While you're getting started, Facebook asks for only a little bit of Profile Information, the part that I like to call the *bio.* Facebook asks for this bio because this is the information that will help your friends find you. The Profile Information step is shown in Figure 1-4.

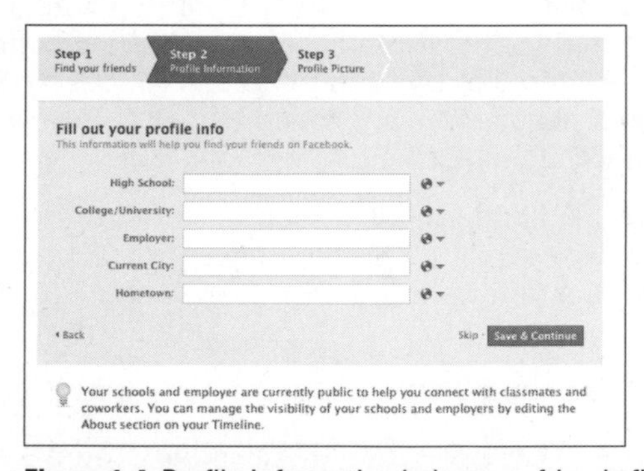

Figure 1-4: Profile Information helps your friends find you.

You can fill out all or none of the five fields, but I definitely recommend filling them all out:

- **High School:** Enter the high school you attended. If you attended more than one high school, pick just one to enter now; you'll be able to add the rest later.
- **College/University:** If you attended college, enter your school. If you attended more than one school, either because you transferred or because you also attended a graduate program, pick one school for now. You'll be able to add the rest later.

- **Employer:** Enter the name of the company you work for. For now, enter wherever you're currently working or where you worked most recently. You'll be able to enter a full work history later.
- **Current City:** Enter the city where you currently reside.
- **Hometown:** Enter the place you identify as your hometown. That may be the place you were born or the place you moved to when you were 10 years old.

You may notice that as you type the name of your high school or college, a list of names appears below the field where you're typing. Get used to seeing these *autocomplete* menus in Facebook. As you type, Facebook tries to guess the rest of the word you're typing. When you see what you're looking for, use the arrow keys to highlight the correct match and press Enter. You'll find similar menus later when you start using search, tagging photos, and sending messages.

Next to each field is a globe icon with an upside-down triangle next to it. This is one version of the Privacy Menu that appears throughout Facebook. Also known as the Audience Selector, you can click this icon to change who can see the information you just entered.

Privacy on Facebook is important. And complex. That's why Chapter 3 is dedicated to understanding it. But for now, decide who can see each of these items. So, for example, if you're choosing privacy for the High School field, you would click the globe icon to open the privacy menu and select from the following options:

- **Public or Everyone:** Anyone who visits your Timeline can see where you went to high school. Additionally, anyone who searches for People Who Went to *<High School Name>* will see you in the search results.
- **Friends:** Only people you add as friends will be able to see where you went to high school.
- **Only Me:** Only you will be able to see where you went to high school. A friend visiting your Timeline won't see this information.
- **Custom:** A specific set of people you choose will or will not be able to see where you went to high school. This option doesn't usually become very useful until people have responded to your Friend Requests.

- **Lists (Close Friends and Family):** Facebook tries to help you sort your friends into categories such as Close Friends or Family (or other types of categories, detailed in Chapter 4). You can choose to allow only people in those lists to see where you went to high school. Much like Custom, this option may not be useful at this time.

If you don't want to share this information publicly, simply click the globe icon and select with whom you do want to share it. Each privacy setting has its own icon to represent it, so if you choose Friends, the globe icon will be replaced by the icon of two silhouettes.

Because these are the fields that help friends find you, I recommend leaving them set to Public. Especially if you have a common name, having some biographical details makes it easier for friends to find and identify you. (Yes, you are the right Jane Smith because you're from Kalamazoo, Michigan.) But if you aren't comfortable with that, you of course can change the privacy setting. Privacy settings aren't set in stone; you can always adjust them (either to make information more or less private) later.

When you're done filling out these fields, click the blue Save & Continue button to move on to the next step.

Sometimes Facebook will use the information you just entered to show you some people it thinks you may know. In that case, after you finish Step 2, but before you get to Step 3, you may see an Add People You Know screen. This screen displays the name and photos of people you may want to add as friends. Click the Add Friend button next to the images of people you know and want to add as friends. You can also choose to skip that part of the step using the Skip link (next to the Save & Continue button).

Step 3: Profile Picture

Much like Step 2, Step 3 is about helping your friends find you, whereas Step 1 was about helping you find them.

Like your biographical information, your profile picture helps set you apart from other people with similar names. Step 3 is shown in Figure 1-5.

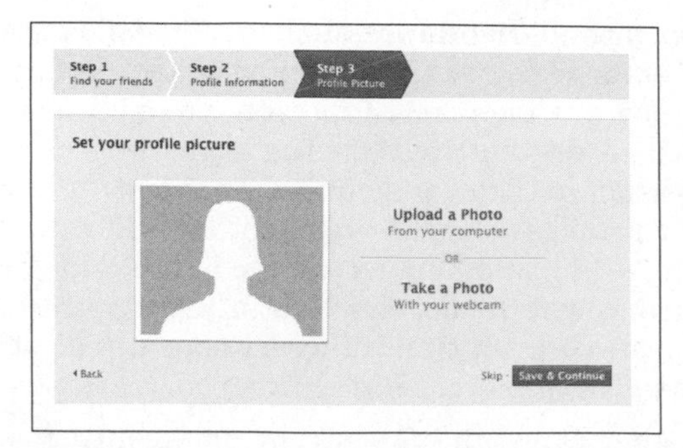

Figure 1-5: Add a profile picture to get your own face on Facebook.

To add your profile picture, make sure you have a photo you want to use saved somewhere on your computer's hard drive, and follow these steps:

1. **Click Upload a Photo.**

   A dialog box like the one shown in Figure 1-6 appears.

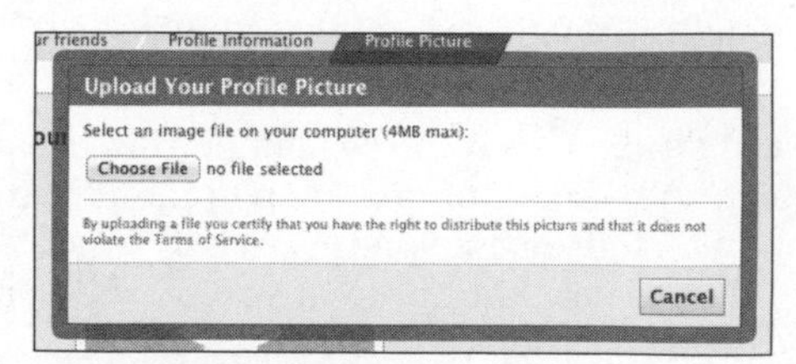

Figure 1-6: Start here to navigate your computer's hard drive.

2. **Click Choose File.**

   Depending on what kind of computer you have, the screen may say something slightly different.

3. **Select your desired photo and click Select or OK.**

   You return to the Getting Started Wizard and a preview of your new profile picture.

4. **Click Save & Continue.**

I talk a lot about your profile picture and the many ways it's used on Facebook in Chapter 2, but here are a few quick tips on selecting a profile picture:

- **Make a good first impression.** Your profile picture is one of the first ways people interact with your Timeline and how you choose to represent yourself. Most people pick pictures that are flattering or that represent what's important to them. Sometimes, profile pictures include other people — friends or significant others. Other times, the location matters. If the first photo you see of someone is at the beach versus at a party or sitting at his desk, you may draw different conclusions about that person. What picture represents you?
- **Consider who will see your profile picture.** By default, your profile picture appears in search results that are visible to all of Facebook and can even be made available to the larger Internet population. So, generally, people who search for your name can see that picture. Make sure it's something you're comfortable with everyone seeing.
- **Pick a photo *you* like.** As you use Facebook, you actually wind up seeing your own photo quite often. Small versions appear wherever you make a comment, post something, or are part of a group. So pick a photo you like looking at.

- **You're not stuck with it.** After I put all this pressure on you to pick the perfect photo, keep in mind that you can easily change your profile picture at any time. Is it the dead of winter, and that photo of you on the beach last summer is just too depressing to look at? No problem; simply edit your profile picture, which you can find out how to do in Chapter 2.

Well, those are pretty much the basics of getting started on Facebook. I hope by now that you've added a few friends, some information about yourself, and a profile picture.

Your New Home Page

After you complete your Getting Started Wizard, you arrive at your Home page. This is where Facebook starts to look like the Facebook you would see if you'd been using the site for a while already. The Home page is what you see when you log in to Facebook.

What's interesting about the Facebook Home page is that while some parts remain the same (such as the big blue bar on top and the menu on the left-hand side), the bulk of what you see is constantly changing. This is because the Home page (also known as the News Feed) updates to show you what your friends are posting, sharing, and talking about on Facebook.

As mentioned, Facebook gets exponentially better once you have friends. This is absolutely true on the Home page. Until your friends respond to your requests, you may not see much here except prompts to learn more about Facebook, find more friends, or fill out information you didn't fill out in Steps 1–3. After you add the people you know as friends, take a break. Your friends may take a few days to respond to your Friend Requests, so be patient. Then come back over the next few days to see the interesting photos, status updates, and links your friends are sharing.

Am I too old for Facebook?

No. Most emphatically, no. This is a common misconception, mainly because Facebook was originally exclusive to college students. Facebook's origins, even its name, are rooted in college campuses, but its utility and nature aren't limited to being useful to only college students.

Everyone has networks of friends and people with whom they interact on a day-to-day basis. Young or old, in college or working, this is true. Facebook tries to map these real-world connections to make it easier for people to share information with their friends.

If you're thinking maybe you're just too old for Facebook, you're wrong. More and more people in older age demographics are signing up for Facebook every day to keep in touch with old friends, share photos, create events, and connect with local organizations. Almost everything I discuss in the book is non-age-specific.

Obviously, how people use the site can be very different at different ages, but you will discover these nuances when you use Facebook more and more. Generally, you should feel confident that you and your friends can connect and use Facebook in a meaningful way.

More than one billion people are using Facebook, and that number isn't made up of "a bunch of kids." Rather, it's a bunch of people from every age group, every country, and every walk of life.

Trust Me: Getting Confirmed and Verified

Facebook is a website for real identity and real people. To protect this fact, Facebook has systems in place to detect any fake accounts. Fake accounts may be jokes (for example, someone creating an account for her dog), or they may be *spammers* (robots creating accounts to send thousands of fake Friend Requests). Regardless, they're not allowed on the site.

You, however, aren't fake or a spammer; how does Facebook know that? Facebook figures that out by confirming and verifying you.

Confirmation

Confirmation is Facebook's way of trying to make sure that you are really you and that the e-mail address you used to sign up is yours. After you finish the earlier three Getting Started steps, you may see a yellow banner across the top of your Home page, asking you to check your e-mail to finish signing up for Facebook.

When you click the Sign Up button (as I describe earlier), Facebook sends you an e-mail asking you to confirm your account. In other words, Facebook is double-checking that you are the person who owns your e-mail address.

To confirm that you are you and that the e-mail address is yours, go to your e-mail, look for that message, and open it. (It will usually have a subject like *Just One More Step to Get Started on Facebook* or *Facebook Confirmation.*) Click the link in that e-mail, and you will be confirmed.

You may have already confirmed your e-mail address by using the Friend Finder or other normal activities. If Facebook isn't bugging you about it with banners or follow-up e-mails, you can pretty much assume you're good to go.

Verification

Verification is a way to make sure that beyond just owning an e-mail account (which, unfortunately, any evil robot can do), you are a real human being who won't abuse Facebook or post inappropriate content. Unfortunately, Facebook has a bit of a "guilty until proven innocent" attitude about all this and puts you through a series of tests to prove your innocence.

Most of these tests aren't ones you have to actively take. Instead, just use the site as your lovely, non-spamming self, and eventually you'll be verified. If you're concerned about being verified right away, however, you can do so by adding a mobile number to your account. Follow these steps:

1. **Click the link on your Home page to add a mobile number.**

   If this link doesn't appear on your Home page, click the gear icon in the top-right corner, select Account Settings, choose Mobile from the left menu, and click the Add a Phone button. A pop-up window appears, as shown in Figure 1-7.

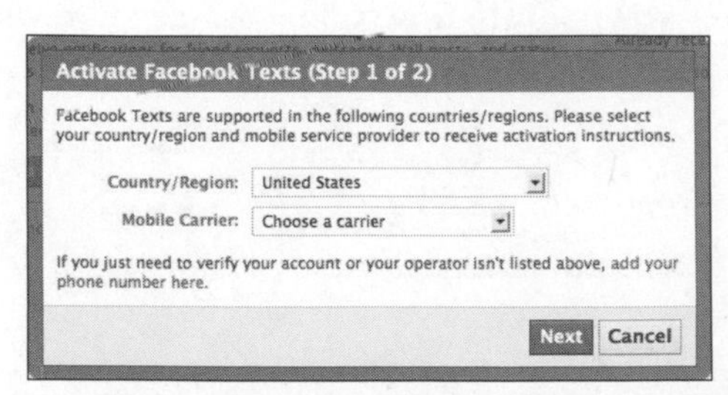

Figure 1-7: Activate Facebook Texts to verify yourself.

   When you add a mobile number, you're signing up for Facebook Texts, a service that will send text messages to your phone to notify you of certain events on Facebook, like receiving a message or getting a Friend Request. If you're not ready to be part of that service (using Facebook on a mobile phone is covered in detail in Chapter 7), you can still verify your account by clicking the blue line of text at the bottom of the window that reads Add Your Phone Number Here.

2. Click the Add Your Phone Number Here link.

This opens the Confirm Your Number window, as shown in Figure 1-8.

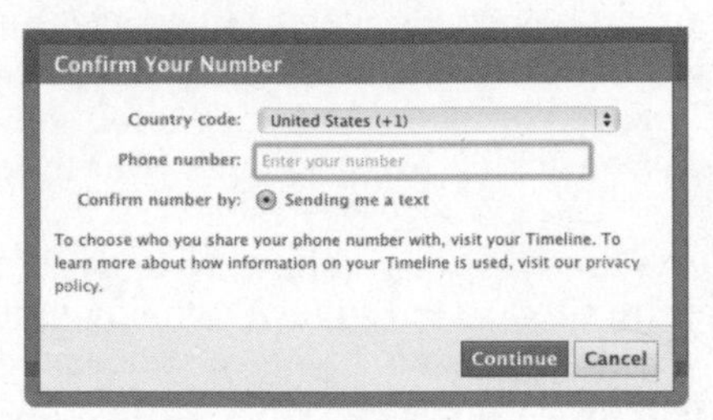

Figure 1-8: Confirm your phone number to prove you're real.

3. Select your country code, enter your phone number in the Phone Number box, and then click Continue.

This sends a text message containing a code to your phone.

4. Back at your computer, enter that code in the designated box on the screen and click Confirm.

After you confirm this code, your account will be verified.

Chapter 2

Timeline: The Story of You

In This Chapter

- Navigating the Timeline
- Filling out and editing your Timeline information
- Sharing with your friends through your Timeline

Your life can change a lot over the course of several years. Looking back and seeing how far you've come is the idea behind the Facebook Timeline. Like many websites, Facebook wants you to establish a profile with the basic biographical information — where you're from, what you do, where you went to school. But in addition to that, Facebook also wants you to keep updating and posting and sharing and marking events that define you. Then it turns all that information into a virtual scrapbook that you and your friends can explore. That virtual scrapbook is your Timeline.

Although Facebook does a lot of the work, this is *your* Timeline, so all aspects of it can be edited, modified, and changed based on how you want to represent yourself and your history. This chapter covers all the ways you edit the information and appearance of your Timeline, as well as who can see what on your Timeline.

Scrolling Through Time

Figure 2-1 shows the top of a Timeline. The Timeline has a few different portions: the big cover photo and the smaller profile picture, the navigation tabs beneath the cover photo, the About box, the Share box, and the Timeline itself, extending from the present back to the day you were born.

Figure 2-1: The top of a Timeline.

In terms of navigating the Timeline, the most important thing to know is that *you scroll down the page to go back in time.* As you scroll down, posts you and your friends have made and life events you have added keep on showing up. When you start scrolling down, a new menu appears at the top of the page (below the blue bar at the top). I call this the *Timeline navigator* (see Figure 2-2).

Figure 2-2: Use the navigator to activate your nostalgia.

The Timeline navigator uses a series of drop-down menus to help you jump around in time. Click any of the buttons to view a drop-down menu of options:

- **Timeline:** This drop-down menu lets you switch from the Timeline itself to the About section of your Timeline. I cover the About section in the "All About Me" section later in this chapter.
- **Year:** This drop-down menu lets you hop from year to year on your Timeline.

- **Highlights/Month:** By default, when you scroll back in time, Facebook shows you *Highlights* — what it thinks are the most important posts or events. You can use the Timeline navigator to change from Highlights to All Stories. When you switch to all stories, you can use this menu to view specific months within a certain year.

First Impressions

If you're new to Facebook, your Timeline may seem empty compared to those of your friends. That's okay; your Timeline will fill up as you start to update your status, post links, and so on. But before you do all that, you want to get the basics filled out so that people can find, recognize, and learn a little bit about you. This section covers the first things people see when they arrive on your Timeline: your cover photo and your profile picture.

The cover photo is the larger photo and serves as a background to your Timeline. People often choose visually striking photos or images that speak to who they are and what they love. To change your cover photo, follow these steps:

1. **Hover your cursor over your existing cover photo, and click the Change Cover button that appears.**

   The Change Cover menu appears with four options: Choose from Photos, Upload Photo, Reposition, and Remove.

   If you're using a Facebook Mobile app that syncs with your phone, you may see an Add Synced Photo option.

2. **Select a cover photo.**

   - To select a photo from photo's you've already added to Facebook, click Choose from Photos.

     The Choose from Your Photos window appears, as shown in Figure 2-3. By default, it shows Recent Uploads. You can get to a full list of your photos by clicking View Albums in the upper-right corner.

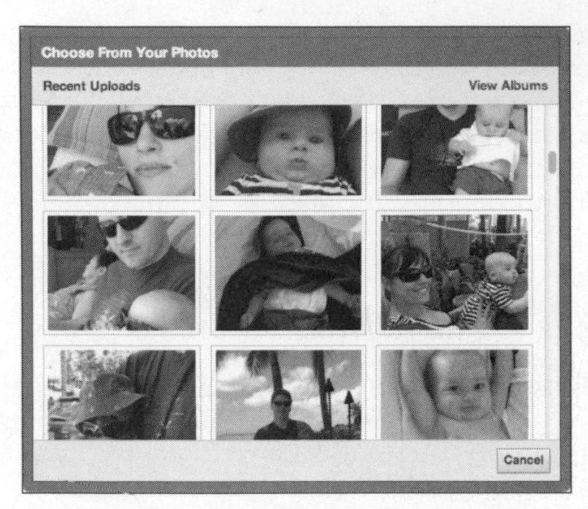

Figure 2-3: Use the Choose from Photos window to choose a cover photo.

- To select a cover photo from your computer, choose Upload Photo.

  A window for navigating your computer's files appears.

3. **Select the photo file you want as your cover and then click Open.**

   You return to your Timeline, where you should see the new cover photo in place with the overlaid message, Drag to Reposition Cover.

   Because the cover photo spans the width of your Timeline, you may occasionally get an error telling you that the photo isn't wide enough. Make sure your cover photo is at least 720 pixels wide.

4. **Drag your cover photo to position it correctly in the frame of the screen.**
5. **Click Save Changes.**

   Your new cover photo is now in place.

If you don't like the way your cover photo is positioned, use the same Change Cover menu to reposition or remove your cover photo. You can change your cover as often as you want.

Your profile picture is the smaller photo. This photo is what sticks with you all around Facebook, appearing wherever you comment or post something. For example, your friends may see your status post in their News Feeds, accompanied by your name and profile picture. Most people use some variation on a headshot for their profile picture. You can add a profile picture in several ways.

Add a profile picture that's already on Facebook

If you skip to Chapter 6, you'll see that Facebook is the number one photo-sharing site on the web, which means there's a good chance someone has already added a photo of you to Facebook that you might like to use as a profile picture.

Use these steps to change your profile picture to one that is already on Facebook:

1. **Hover your cursor over your existing profile picture, and then click the Edit Profile Picture button.**

   The Profile Picture menu appears.

2. **To choose from the photos of you on Facebook, click Choose from Photos.**

   The Choose from Photos window appears, which by default shows you all the photos that you're tagged in on Facebook. Page through these photos by clicking the arrows in the bottom-right corner. You can also get to the photos you've added to Facebook by clicking View Albums in the upper-right corner.

3. **Click the photo you want as your profile picture.**

   The photo appears with a cropping interface, as shown in Figure 2-4.

4. **Using the cropping functions, choose the portion of the photo you want as your profile picture.**

   Move the transparent box around the photo by clicking and dragging it. Click and drag the corners of the transparent box to resize.

5. **Click Done Cropping when you've finished.**

   You return to your Timeline, with the new profile picture visible.

Figure 2-4: Crop profile pictures to focus on just you.

Add a profile picture from your hard drive

If there aren't any photos on Facebook that would make suitable profile pictures, you can choose a photo from your computer's hard drive:

1. **Hover the cursor over your existing profile picture.**
2. **Click the Edit Profile Picture button, and then select Upload Photo.**
3. **Locate and select the desired photo.**
4. **Click Open or Choose.**

   The photo is added and appears in place of your old profile picture.

Take a photo of yourself using your webcam

If you have a camera built into your computer or an external webcam, you can also take a photo to be your profile picture by following these steps:

1. **Hover the cursor over your existing profile picture, and then click the Edit Profile Picture button that appears.**

   The Profile Picture menu appears.

2. **Select Take Photo.**

   An interface for shooting a photo using your computer's webcam appears.

3. **Click the button at the bottom of the screen to take your photo.**

   Remember to smile!

4. **If you're happy with the photo, click Save as Profile Picture.**

   The photo is added and appears in place of your old profile picture.

You can change your profile picture as often as you choose. Every photo you select as your profile picture is automatically added to the Profile Pictures album.

Your cover photo and profile picture are visible to anyone who searches for you and clicks on your name. Make sure you're comfortable with everyone seeing these images.

Telling Your Story

Getting back to the main focus of your Timeline, look at the stuff below the cover photo. Two columns run down the page:

- The skinny column on the left side is full of interests, recent activity, and application activity. (I cover these parts of your Timeline in the upcoming "Sections" section.)
- The wider right column is where posts and life events live. These posts might be something you've added to Facebook, like a status, or something someone has added to Facebook about you, like a photo tag. These posts constitute your Timeline. As you scroll down your past, you can see what you were posting last week, last month, last year.

Whether you joined Facebook yesterday or five years ago, you can use Facebook to highlight important events in your life that are happening now or in years past. This section goes over the basics of sharing your story, from the ongoing process of status updates and photo posts to the posting of life events to the capability to curate your Timeline to highlight your favorite posts and events.

Adding posts

Posts are the type of sharing you'll be doing most often on Facebook. People post multiple times a day about an array of topics. They post things from the Share box, also known as the Publisher. The Share box is the text field at the top of your Timeline's right column, as shown in Figure 2-5.

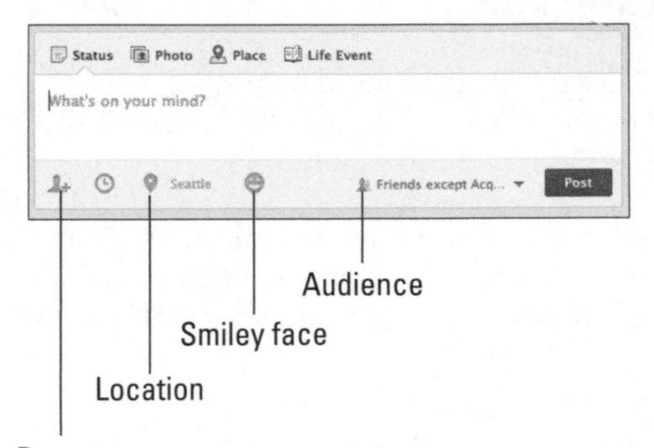

Figure 2-5: The Share box on the Timeline.

The Share box is what you use to post content — statuses, photos, places, links, and so on — to your Timeline. When you post content, you can also choose who can see it. Friends and subscribers then may see these posts in their News Feeds when they log in. (For more information on News Feed, check out Chapter 5.)

Status section

The most common type of post that you see people make from the Share box is a basic text update that answers the question, "What's on your mind?" On Facebook, people refer to this type of post as a *status update* or just as their *status.* Status updates are quick, short, and completely open to interpretation. People may update them with what they may be doing at that moment ("Eating a snack"), offer a random observation ("A cat in my backyard just caught a snake!"), or request info ("Planning a trip to India this summer. Anyone know where I should stay?"). It's easy for friends to comment on statuses, so a provocative update can really get the conversation going. I comment on commenting in Chapter 5.

To update your status, follow these steps:

1. **Click the What's on Your Mind field of the Share box.**

   This step expands the Share box.

2. **Type your comment, thought, or status.**

3. **(Optional) Click the person icon in the bottom gray bar of the Share box to add tags to your post.**

   Tags are ways of marking people you're with when you're writing a status update. The tags link back to your friends' Timelines and notify them of your update. When you tag someone, an additional bit of text is added to the status, so it looks like this: *Off to play board games — with Eric.* Eric then receives a notification that you tagged him.

4. **(Optional) Click the location pin icon to add a location.**

   Facebook Places is a feature I cover in Chapter 6. You can click this pin and begin typing a city or place name, and Facebook tries to autocomplete the place where you are. Letting friends know where you are (called *checking in*) is a great way to increase the chances of serendipitous encounters.

5. **(Optional) Click the smiley face icon to add info about what you're doing, interacting with, or feeling.**

   Much like tagging a person or checking in to a location, you can add details to your status about what you're reading, watching, feeling, doing, and so on. Facebook attempts to autocomplete things as you type.

6. **(Optional) Click the audience menu in the bottom-right corner to change who can see this post.**

   You can choose from the basic privacy options: Public, Friends, Friends Except Acquaintances, Only Me, and Custom. Your selection is saved for your next status post. For example, if I post a link to Friends, the next time I go to update my status, Facebook assumes I also want to share that with Friends.

7. **Click Post.**

If that made you feel like updating your status requires way too much work, remember that many steps are optional. You can follow the abridged version of the preceding if you prefer:

1. **Click in the Share box.**
2. **Type your status.**
3. **Click Post.**

Frequently, people use their status updates to bring attention to something else on the Internet, such as an article or an event. Usually, people add a comment to explain the link; other times, they use the link itself as their status.

To post a link, simply follow the instructions for updating a status and copy and paste the link you want into the field where you normally type a status. This automatically expands a preview of your post, as shown in Figure 2-6.

Figure 2-6: A preview of your post.

A preview usually contains a headline, a thumbnail photo, and teaser text. Hover your cursor over either the headline or teaser text and click to edit what appears in the preview. Use the arrows at the bottom of the preview to change the thumbnail. You can also edit your own comment.

If you delete the URL text from the Share box, it doesn't actually remove the link from your post. In fact, deleting the link can make your post look cleaner and leave more room for your own thoughts about the link.

Photo section

Facebook is the Internet's number-one photo-sharing website. In other words, people love to share photos, and they post a lot of them on Facebook. Consider this fact a teaser trailer for Chapter 6, where I go over the entire Photo application, including adding photos from the Share box.

Place section

The third type of post that Facebook gives you a special tab for within the Share box is a place check-in. Typically, check-ins are part of another post, like a status, but if all you want to do is note where you are, click Place and start typing the name of your location. You can also add tags or a comment to your check-in. Click Post when you're done.

Life Events section

Part of what's nice about Facebook is the way it lets you connect with friends over the small stuff: a nice sunset on your walk home, a funny observation in the park (cats in strollers! Hilarious!). But Facebook is also awesome for letting you connect over the big stuff. Babies being born, houses being purchased, pets being adopted. The milestones, if you will. The Life Events section lets you make a note of that event on your Timeline.

If you're new to Facebook, you may want to expand your Timeline back past the day you joined. To add a life event, follow these steps:

1. **Click the Life Event section in the Share box.**

   A menu of various types of life events appears along with many subcategories.

Milestones can be big or small; if you check out the subcategories, you'll see things that range from getting your braces removed to learning a new hobby to having a baby. Feel free to make up your own.

2. **Select the event you want to create.**

   A pop-up window appears with fields to fill out and space for photos, as shown in Figure 2-7.

Figure 2-7: Add a life event from the recent or distant past.

3. **Fill out the details you want to share.**

   You don't have to fill out all the fields, but it's important to fill in the date of the event so that it goes to the right place on your Timeline.

4. **Add a photo to illustrate the event.**

   Click Choose from Photos if you want to use a photo already on Facebook, or click Upload Photos to add photos from your computer.

5. **Use the Privacy menu to choose who can see this event in your Timeline.**

6. **Click Save.**

   The event is added to your Timeline, with any photos you've added featured prominently.

As you scroll down through your history, you may realize that you want to add an event or milestone. Don't worry about scrolling back to the top of the page. The Timeline navigator should be following you as you scroll down, showing your name and the year you're looking at. Click the Life Event icon on the right side of this bar to add a milestone to your past.

Editing posts

If you've been on Facebook for a while and start scrolling backward through time, you may notice that you're not actually seeing everything. Facebook attempts to create a *Highlights,* or selections of the best posts to represent your history. But Facebook doesn't always get it right, so you can always go back and choose your own highlights.

Hover your cursor over any post in your Timeline to reveal two icons in the upper-right corner (see Figure 2-8). The star icon allows you to highlight a post. Highlighting it puts a little blue flag over the corner of the post. Click that flag again to remove the highlight.

Figure 2-8: Highlight, edit, or remove a post.

Click the pencil icon to edit the post. You can change the date, change the location, hide the post from the Timeline, or delete it. These options are available only for your own posts. For posts that your friends have left on your Timeline, you can change the date and hide the post from Timeline. You can also delete or report posts left on your wall.

Photo posts contain an additional option: Reposition Photo. Because the post boxes are uniform sizes, sometimes photos get cropped on your Timeline. Click this option to reposition which section of a photo is seen in the post on your Timeline.

Hiding a post is different from deleting it. When you hide a post, you keep that post from appearing on your Timeline, but the post still exists. So if, for example, you hide a particularly bad photo from your Timeline, the photo album still exists. Anyone with permission to see it could navigate to your Photos section and check it out. But it's not going to get called out on your Timeline. If you delete a post, it's gone forever; even you won't be able to find it on Facebook.

If you're looking to remove things like photos or videos that exist only on Facebook, keep in mind that once they're gone from Facebook, they're gone forever. It might be more practical to change the audience that can see the photo album than to delete it entirely. Trust me; one hard-drive crash, and your photos are Facebook-only.

Sections

Whereas the right column of your Timeline is dedicated to posts and life events, the left column is for everything else. This includes some biographical information about you, your interests, your friends, previews of your photos, and recent activity on Facebook. Represented as a series of boxes, Facebook refers to these as *sections.* I like to think of sections as compilations of information. You might become friends with one new person per month and be tagged in three photos. Rather than take up space on the right side of your Timeline and overshadow the very interesting posts, this information is instead compiled in a Recent Activity box on the left side. Here are a few of the sections you may see on your Timeline:

- **About:** The About box shows only a portion of the information you may have added to your About section. The part it does show includes the things that help identify you as you.

  These pieces of info — where you work, where you live, who your spouse is — are the sorts of things you might talk about the first time you meet someone.

- **Friends:** The Friends box shows thumbnail photos of, you guessed it, your friends. Usually, friends you recently added will appear here, and as you scroll back in time, this box highlights whom you added when.
- **Photos:** The Photos box shows thumbnails of photos you've been tagged in, starting with the most recent one. When you scroll back in time, it will show other details about the photos from that time.
- **Places:** The Places box displays locations where you've checked in recently. As you scroll back in time, it shows a

map of all the places you checked in at that time period, and usually highlights one in particular on the map.

- **Activity:** The Activity box (shown in Figure 2-9) highlights actions you've taken on Facebook that aren't posts, such as people you've become friends with or an event you attended. As you scroll back in time, this box reappears to give summaries of, for example, how many friends you added last year.

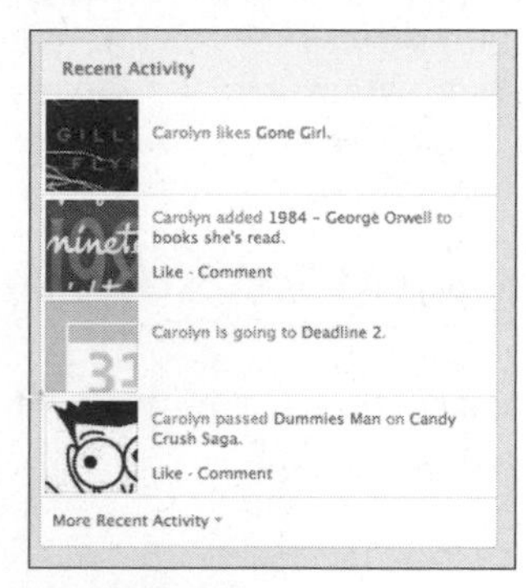

Figure 2-9: Recent activity shows what you've been up to.

- **Likes:** The Likes box shows pages that you've liked, starting with the most recent one. As you scroll back in time, this box shows pages you liked at particular times.
- **Interests:** Multiple interest boxes are available for things like music, movies, and books. In theory, these are filled out as you add information to your posts. For example, if you post that you're reading *The Great Gatsby* and tag that book using the @ symbol, *The Great Gatsby* is added to the Books box.
- **Application Activity:** Here, an *application* refers to a website, a game, or another program that allows you to integrate some aspect of Facebook into it. For example, you can integrate Facebook into Spotify, a music-streaming program, so your friends can see what you are listening to.

  Many applications have some aspect of automatic sharing, so after you sign up, every time you take a certain action — reading articles on *The Washington Post,* watching a TV show on Hulu — that activity will be added to your Timeline. This sort of activity gets its own box with info about the application you used.

If you don't want activity published to your Timeline from a particular application, you can always hide that app's section. Hover the cursor over the recent activity box from that app, click the pencil icon that appears, and select Hide Section. You can learn more about controlling your apps in Chapter 8.

Adding to your interest sections

Interest sections are a part of the Timeline that can be a really fun way to let your friends know the music, movies, television shows, books, and other things that really define you. You can share books you have read and your favorite books with your Facebook friends by following these steps (the same steps apply to the other Interest sections):

1. **Click the More link below your cover photo and select Books from the drop-down menu.**

   The expanded Books section of your Timeline appears, as shown in Figure 2-10.

Figure 2-10: An expanded Books section on your Timeline.

2. **Click the section to which you want to add books.**

   You can add books to three sections: Read, Want to Read, and Likes.

3. **In the Search box, type the name of the book you want to add.**

Facebook attempts to autocomplete as you type. When you see the book you want to add, click it or press Enter. You may also be able to click from a selection of suggested books that Facebook displays.

4. **Repeat Step 3 as needed.**

Editing sections

You can decide which compilation boxes appear on your Timeline as well as the order they appear as you scroll down. To edit which sections appear and how they show up, hover your cursor over any of the Interest boxes in the left column; then click the blue pencil icon that appears in the upper-right corner of that box. If you do this with the Movies box, for example, you'll see the following options:

- **Edit Sections:** View a list of all possible sections. Deselect the ones you don't want, and drag the other sections to change their order.

  Make sure you click Save when you're done.
- **Hide Section:** Hide the Movies section on your Timeline.
- **Activity Log:** See all activity (Activity Log) related to movies that could appear in the Movies box.
- **Edit Privacy:** Edit who can see all the movies you have liked on Facebook.

All About Me

The About box gives you (and your friends) the dinner party basics: where you live, what you do, where you're from, whom you're with. But there's a lot more information about you that Facebook gives you the opportunity to share. Clicking the About link beneath your cover photo opens the expanded About section of your Timeline (see Figure 2-11).

This page houses lots of information about you: Work and Education, Basic Information, Living, Relationships and Family, Contact Information. Much of this information won't change much over time, so it needs to be edited only once or when something big happens, like you move to a new city.

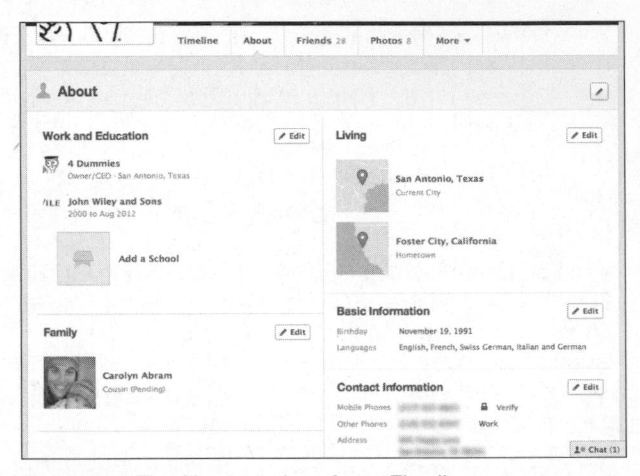

Figure 2-11: The About section of your Timeline.

You can visit the About section to edit this information as well as edit who can see it. Unlike the cover photo and profile picture, you choose who gets to see this information. By default, your information is public, meaning everyone can see it, but five privacy options are available:

- **Public or Everyone:** Anyone who finds your Timeline, potentially anywhere on the Internet, can see this piece of information. Use this setting for things that are not personal or are already public knowledge.

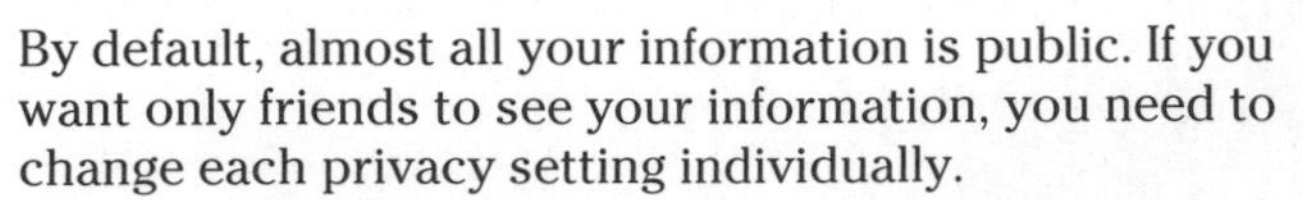

By default, almost all your information is public. If you want only friends to see your information, you need to change each privacy setting individually.

- **Friends:** Only your friends can see that piece of information. This setting is useful for more personal things like your contact information.
- **Friends Except Acquaintances:** This option refers to the "acquaintances" smart list that Facebook creates for many users. People who have been added to this list will be unable to see this information.
- **Only Me:** Keep information on your Timeline for your own reference but do not show it to anyone else.

- **Custom:** Use custom settings to show items to specific groups of people. You can choose a setting like Friends of Friends if you want something to be visible to more than just friends, but not to the public. You can even choose to show something only to specific friends or to hide it from specific friends. For more on these privacy options and how to use them, check out Chapter 3.

All information fields in the About section are optional. If something doesn't apply to you, or you don't want to share that information, just leave it blank.

Work and Education

Remember when Facebook asked you to enter your education and work history? If you didn't do that or want to add a more complete online resume, you can add more schools and employers on the Work and Education page. This information can help old friends find you for reunions, recommendations, or reminiscing. From the About section of the Timeline, click the Edit button in the upper-right corner of the Work and Education section. You can then add and edit professional and educational information. When you're finished, click the Done Editing button in the upper-right corner.

See the little privacy icon to the right of the Where Have You Worked field? Click that icon to change who can see this information. Almost every field in the About section has a privacy icon.

To add an employer, follow these steps:

1. **After you click the Edit button, click the Where Have You Worked? field.**
2. **Start typing the name of the company where you worked or currently work.**

   Facebook tries to find a match while you type. When that match is highlighted, or when you finish typing, press Enter.

3. **Enter details about your job:**
   - *Position:* Your job title.
   - *City/Town:* Where you physically went (or go) to work.
   - *Description:* A more detailed description of what you do.
   - *Time Period:* The amount of time you worked at this job. If you select I Currently Work Here, it appears at the top of your Timeline.
4. **Click Add Job.**
5. **Either add more jobs or click Done Editing in the upper-right corner.**

   You can change any of the information about this job (or others) later by clicking its Edit link.

If you're interested in using Facebook for professional networking, you can also add specific projects to your work history.

To add a high school or college, follow these steps:

1. **Click the Where Did You Go to High School (or College)? field.**
2. **Start typing the name of the school you attended (or attend).**

   Facebook tries to find a match while you type. When that match is highlighted, or when you finish typing, press Enter.
3. **Enter details of your school:**
   - *Time Period:* Click the blue text Add Year to show when you started and finished your degree.
   - *Graduated:* (High school only) Select this box if you graduated from this school.
   - *Description:* Add details about your time at school that you think may be relevant.
   - *Concentrations:* List any majors or minors you had.

- *Attended For:* (College only) Choose whether you attended as an undergraduate or a graduate student. If you select Graduate Student, you can enter the type of degree you received.

4. **Click Add School.**

You can edit any of this information by clicking the Edit link next to the employer or school you want to edit.

When you're done adding and editing your professional and educational history, click Done Editing to save your changes.

Living

The Living section contains two pins on two maps: one to show where you're from, and one to show your current city. Click Edit to change either of these and to control who can see this information. Remember to click Save when you're done.

Basic Information

Your Basic Information is what it sounds like: the very basics about you that you might use to identify who you are and where you're from. Click Edit to open a window where you can edit these fields and who can see them.

By default, your basic information (with the exception of your birthday) is public. Change your privacy settings using the drop-down menu to the right of each item in the list.

- **Sex (I Am):** You entered your sex when you signed up for Facebook, and it mirrors your selection here. If you don't want people to see your sex on your Timeline, deselect the check box below this field.
- **Birthday:** You also entered your birthday when you registered for Facebook. Here, you can tweak the date (in case you messed up) as well as decide what people can see about your birthday. Use this drop-down menu to select what you want to share.

Although you can change your birthday and year most of the time, Facebook's systems prevent you from shifting to under 18 after you've been listed as over 18. If you've made a legitimate mistake, contact Facebook's User Operations team from the Help Center.

- **Interested In:** This field is primarily used by people to signal their sexual orientation. Some people feel that this section makes Facebook seem like a dating site, so if that doesn't sound like you, you don't have to fill it out.
- **Relationship Status:** You can edit who, if anyone, you're seeing, and what type of relationship you're in both here and in the Relationship section.
- **Languages:** You can enter any languages you speak here.
- **Religion:** You can choose to list your religion and describe it.
- **Political Views:** You can also choose to list and explain your political views.

When you edit a section of your information, click the Save button so you don't lose your work.

Relationship and Family

The Relationship section and the Family section provide space for you to list your romantic and family relationships. These relationships provide a way of linking your Timeline to someone else's Timeline, and therefore require confirmation. In other words, if you list yourself as married, your spouse needs to confirm that fact before it appears on both Timelines.

You can add a relationship by following these steps:

1. **Click the Edit button in the upper-right corner of the Relationship section.**

   A pop-up window for editing this information appears.

2. **Click the Relationship Status menu and select a relationship.**
3. **(Optional) Link to the person you're in this relationship with by typing the person's name in the box that appears.**

   Facebook autocompletes as you type. Press Enter when you see your beloved's name highlighted. This sends a notification to that person.

4. **(Optional) Add your anniversary using the drop-down menus that appear.**

If you add your anniversary, your friends will see a small reminder on their Home pages on that date.

5. **Click Save.**

For many couples, the act of changing from Single to In a Relationship on Facebook is a major relationship milestone. There's even a term for it: Facebook official. You may overhear someone saying, "It's official, but is it Facebook official?" Feel free to impress your friends with this knowledge of Facebook customs.

To add a family relationship, follow these steps:

1. **Click the Edit button in the upper-right corner of the Family section.**

   A pop-up window for editing this information appears.

2. **Click the text box for Family Member and start typing your family member's name.**

   Facebook tries to autocomplete as you type. When your sister's or mother's or whomever's name appears, click to select it.

3. **Select the type of relationship from the drop-down menu.**

   Facebook offers a variety of family relationships ranging from the nuclear to the extended.

4. **Click Save at the bottom of the pop-up window.**

Contact Information

I know, it may seem a little scary to add your contact information to the Internet, and if you're not comfortable with it, that's okay. Facebook itself is a great way for people to reach you, so you don't have to add other ways for people to contact you as well.

That said, it can be useful for your friends to have your number or address, and privacy options can help you feel more comfortable sharing some of this information. (See the end of this chapter for more information on Timeline privacy.) To edit your contact information, follow these steps:

1. **Click the Edit button in the upper-right corner of the Contact Information section.**

   A pop-up window for editing this information appears.

2. **Click the respective text fields for adding e-mail addresses, phone numbers, IM handles, addresses, and websites.**

   If you've already added any of these and want to add more, look for the links to Add Another.

3. **Enter the appropriate information.**

4. **Click Save.**

Your Friends and Your Timeline

Your Timeline is what your friends look at to get a sense of your life, and it's also where they leave public messages for you. In this way, your friends' posts become part of your history (just like in real life).

When friends visit your Timeline, they'll also see a version of the Share box that you see. They can't add life events, but they can post text and photos to your Timeline. Check out the posts on your friends' Timelines. Chances are that you'll see a few "Hey, how are you, let's catch up" messages; a few "That was an awesome dinner" messages; and maybe a few statements that make so little sense, you're sure they must be inside jokes.

If you're on a friend's Timeline around his birthday, you're sure to see many "Happy Birthday" posts. Because most people see notifications of their friends' birthdays on their Home pages, the quickest way to say "I'm thinking of you" on their special day is to write on their Timeline.

Although I think that the back and forth between friends is one of the delights of the Timeline, some people find it a little hard to let go. To prevent friends from being able to post on your Timeline or to limit who can see the posts your friends leave, change the options in the Timeline and Tagging section of the Settings page.

Chapter 3

Privacy and Safety

In This Chapter

- Navigating the many privacy options on Facebook
- Protecting yourself online and on Facebook
- Deciding what to share and when

When people talk about privacy online — and on Facebook in particular — I like to remind them that there's a spectrum of privacy concerns. On one end of the spectrum are true horror stories of predators approaching minors, identity thefts, and the like. I hope you will never deal with these issues. On the other end of the spectrum are "awkward social situations" — for example, posting a photo of your perfect beach day that your co-workers can see on a day when you called in "sick." Somewhere in between are questions about strangers seeing your stuff and security issues like spamming and phishing. All these privacy-related topics are legitimate, though you'll probably deal with the awkward end of the spectrum more often than anything else. The goal is to get as close to 100 percent as possible so you can feel as comfortable as possible sharing on Facebook.

There's also a spectrum of what "being comfortable" means: What makes me comfortable might not make you comfortable. This chapter is meant to be a guide to Facebook's privacy options so that you can figure out the right combinations that make you comfortable sharing on Facebook.

Your own common sense is going to be one of the best helpers in avoiding privacy problems.

Knowing Your Audience

Before getting into specifics about the privacy controls, you need to understand some basic parts of the Facebook vocabulary. These terms are related to how Facebook thinks about the people you may or may not want to share with. For most pieces of information, the privacy options are related to the audience who can see what you're sharing. Each is represented by its own icon:

- **Public or Everyone:** By setting the visibility of something you post or list to Public, you're saying that you don't care who, on the entire Internet, knows this information about you. Many people list their spouse on their Timeline and — just as they'd shout this information from the treetops — set the visibility to Public. This setting is reasonable for innocuous pieces of information. Some information — including your name, current profile picture, gender, your username, and your cover image — is always available as Public information that everyone can see.

  Now, just because everyone *can* see something doesn't mean everyone *does* see everything. Your posts, information, friendships, and so on, populate your friends' News Feeds (assuming that your friends can see this information), but never the News Feeds of people you're not friends with (unless you allow subscribers to see your public posts). By default, much of your Timeline and all your posts are publicly visible. This chapter covers how to change these settings.

- **Friends:** Any information for which you set visibility to Friends will be accessible only by your confirmed Facebook friends. If you trust your friends, this is a reasonably safe setting for most of your information. If you feel uncomfortable sharing your information with your friends, you can use Custom privacy, or you can rethink the people you allow to be your friends.

Think of friending people as its own privacy setting. When you add someone as a friend, ask yourself whether you're comfortable with that person seeing your posts.

- **Friends Except Acquaintances:** Even though I always recommend adding friends only if you're comfortable with them seeing your posts, this setting forces me to acknowledge that sometimes you have not-quite-friends on your Friend list. These may be distant family members, professional contacts, old friends from way back when, or that super-friendly neighbor whom you maybe just wish wouldn't stop by quite so often. No matter who they are, you can add them to the Acquaintances list and then use this setting to limit what they can see about you.
- **Only Me:** This setting is basically a way of adding something to Facebook but then hiding it from other people. I can't think of many times I've found this setting useful, except when I start something like adding a photo album, and want to come back later to finish it.
- **Custom:** If you have specific needs, customized privacy settings may help you feel more comfortable sharing on Facebook. The Custom privacy option allows you to choose specific people (or lists of people) who can see something, or choose specific people (or lists of people) who can't see something.
- **Lists:** Lists are ways to sort your friends into various categories. The two types of lists are Smart Lists, which Facebook creates on your behalf, and lists that you create yourself. For example, Facebook creates the Family list based on information you enter about your family relationships. I've created a "Dummies" list to keep track of the various editors and co-authors I've had over the years. Often, you may want to share something with one particular list of people, in which case you can choose the name of that list as your privacy setting.

Privacy When Sharing

Privacy on Facebook isn't a one-time thing. Because you're constantly adding new status updates, photos, and content to Facebook, constantly interacting with friends and reaching out to people, privacy is an ongoing affair. To that end, one of the most common places where you should know your privacy options is in the Share box.

The *Share box* is the blank text box that sits at the top of your Home page and below your cover photo on your Timeline. It's where you go to add status updates, photos, links, and more to Facebook. The part of the Share box that's important for this chapter is the Privacy menu, right next to the Post button, as shown in Figure 3-1.

Figure 3-1: Use the Privacy menu to adjust privacy for an individual post.

Whenever you're posting a status or other content, the *audience,* or group of people you've given permission to see it, is displayed next to the blue Post button. The audience you see displayed is always the audience you last shared something with. In other words, if you shared something with Public last time you posted a status, it displays Public the next time you go to post a status.

Hovering your cursor over this word turns it into a button. Click that button to reveal the drop-down menu shown in Figure 3-1. Additionally, if you use Friend Lists, commonly used ones appear below the usual privacy options (check out Chapter 4 for more about Friend Lists). Click the setting you want before you post your status, link, or photo. Most of the time, I share my posts with friends. As a result, I don't actually change this setting that often. But if you do share something publicly, remember to adjust the audience the next time you post something.

Sometimes, you may find that you want to share something with only a portion of your friends. To do that, choose Custom from the Privacy menu. The Custom Privacy window appears, as shown in Figure 3-2.

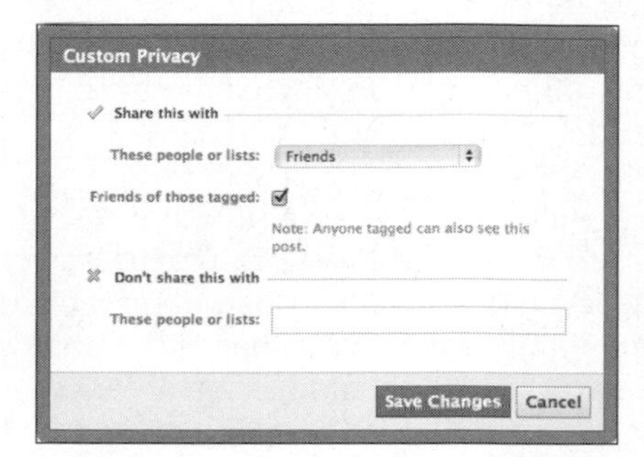

Figure 3-2: Customize your privacy down to the person.

Custom Privacy here applies to the post you're creating, but this dialog box appears any time you choose Custom as a privacy setting for any type of information. Customized privacy has two parts: those who *can* see something and those who *can't*. The top portion controls the former and has four options:

- **Friends of Friends:** Your friends and their friends can see whatever you post.
- **Friends:** Only your friends can see what you post.
- **Specific People or Lists:** Only the people you enter in the blank text box that appears can see your post.
- **Only Me:** Only you can see the post.

Additionally, when you choose the Friends of Friends option or the Friends option, a check box allows you to choose whether the friends of any people you tag can see your post. Remember, tagging is a way of marking who is in a photo, who is with you when you check in someplace, or who you want to mention in a post. For example, if I post a status that says "Taking advantage of the nice weather with Kate," the name of my friend, Kate, links back to her profile. By default, Kate's friends will be able to see this post, even if they aren't friends with me. If I deselect this box, Kate's friends will no longer be able to see that post.

The lower section of the Custom Privacy window controls who can't see something. Similar to the Specific People or Lists setting, the Don't Share This With section has a blank text box where you can type the name of people or lists of people. When you add their names to this box, they won't be able to see the content you post.

Whatever customized audience you create for one post will be the audience next time you go to post something. Make sure you check the audience the next time you post!

People can hover their cursor over a post's privacy icon (Public, Friends of Friends, Friends, or Custom) to get more information. Friend Lists appear as Custom privacy unless the viewer is a member of a list you shared the post with. Members of a default (Close Friends, Acquaintances) or custom Friend List can see other people included on the list but are unable to see the name of the list.

After you post something, you can always change its privacy. From your Timeline, follow these steps:

1. **Hover your mouse over the privacy icon at the top of the post whose audience you want to change.**
2. **Click the button to reveal the Privacy menu.**
3. **Click the audience you want.**

   A change to any audience except Custom is automatically saved. Changing to Custom requires you to make selections in the Custom Privacy window again.

Privacy Shortcuts

Facebook has so many settings related to privacy that the topic can feel overwhelming. I'm a fan of the Privacy Shortcuts menu, which helps direct you to the settings you'll want most often by asking the questions you'll ask most often:

- Who can see my stuff?
- Who can contact me?
- How do I stop someone from bothering me?

To open the Privacy Shortcuts menu, shown in Figure 3-3, click the lock icon next to your profile picture in the left sidebar (remember, you may have to hover your cursor over the left sidebar to expand it). Click any of the three options to expand more privacy options.

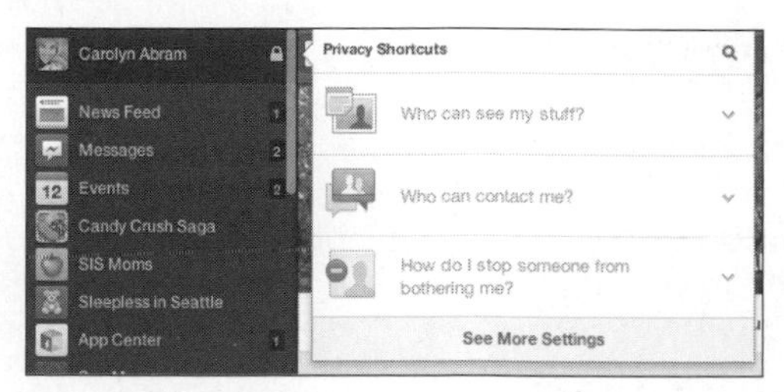

Figure 3-3: You can find the answers to your most common privacy questions here.

Who can see my stuff?

You can adjust the privacy for each status or post you make, which means that over time you might find yourself asking, "Wait, who can see all of this? Who can see what I posted yesterday? Last week? What about if I post tomorrow?" Well, the answers can be found here. (The earlier "Privacy When Sharing" section of this chapter covers the privacy options when you're sharing something.)

Facebook offers you one setting you can adjust here, named Who Can See My Future Posts. This is the same control that can be found in the Share box. It's described this way to emphasize that whatever you select here will be the default going forward, until you change it again. Click the little arrow to change this setting.

Additionally, the Who Can See My Stuff section offers you two links to help you double-check and understand what people can see. The first is a link to Activity Log, which is a granular summary of everything you've done on Facebook and who can see that thing. It ranges from the status updates you write to the content you like or comment on. As you look through your Activity Log, you can change who can see it, or remove the content entirely. I go over how to navigate and edit your Activity Log in more depth in the "Privacy Tools" section later in this chapter.

Finally, the Who Can See My Stuff section offers you a link to another privacy tool, the View As tool. This tool allows you to look at your Timeline as though you are another person. I like to use this to double-check what people see when they search for me on Facebook.

Who can contact me?

A common Facebook problem that sends people scurrying to their privacy settings is getting a message or Friend Request that they don't want to get. It might be from a spammer or just someone you don't know. The Who Can Contact Me section is to help you control which messages you see and who can send you Friend Requests.

The first option in this section provides the filtering options for your Messages Inbox. (Facebook Inbox automatically sorts your messages to prioritize ones from friends.) The two filter options are

- **Basic Filtering:** This option, which is the default, shows you messages from friends as well as messages from people Facebook thinks you might know. They could be friends of friends or other people Facebook's algorithms have determined you might know. These messages will appear in your Inbox.
- **Strict Filtering:** This filter option means the messages from friends of friends and people you may know go to a separate section of your Inbox where you're not as likely to see them.

Regardless of what you choose, some messages will always go to the Other Messages section of your Inbox: messages Facebook thinks might be spam or those in which you have no connection to the person sending it. The Strict filtering option just means you never get a message from someone you don't know in your main box.

The second control in this section concerns who can send you Friend Requests: Everyone and Friends of Friends. Everyone means that everyone who searches for you or finds your Timeline can add you as a friend. Friends of Friends means someone has to be friends with one of your friends before he's allowed to request you.

How do I stop someone from bothering me?

Sadly, sometimes a friendship isn't really a friendship. If someone is bothering, harassing, or bullying you, or in any way making your Facebook experience terrible, blocking might be the solution to the problem. Blocking is different than unfriending someone because someone who is not your friend might still wind up interacting with you on Facebook. For example, if you have mutual friends, you might wind up both commenting on the same post. Blocking someone means that as much as possible, neither of you will even know that the other person is on Facebook. You won't see each other's comments, even if they're on the same person's photo. They won't be able to send you messages, add you as a friend, or view your Timeline (all things they would likely be able to do even if you unfriended them).

If you're the parent of a teen, this can be a handy setting. Blocking can be a useful tool in terms of keeping your child from bullies on Facebook.

Privacy Settings

In addition to the privacy shortcuts, several more granular privacy settings are located in the Settings page. You can get to these settings from the Privacy Shortcuts menu (click the See More Settings link).

The Privacy Settings and Tools section of the Settings page is shown in Figure 3-4. The left side of the Settings page is a menu of settings you can adjust here. The settings that are relevant to privacy are in the second section: Privacy, Timeline and Tagging, and Blocking. I also go over the Apps and Ads settings sections because people commonly have questions about how their information is used in these locations.

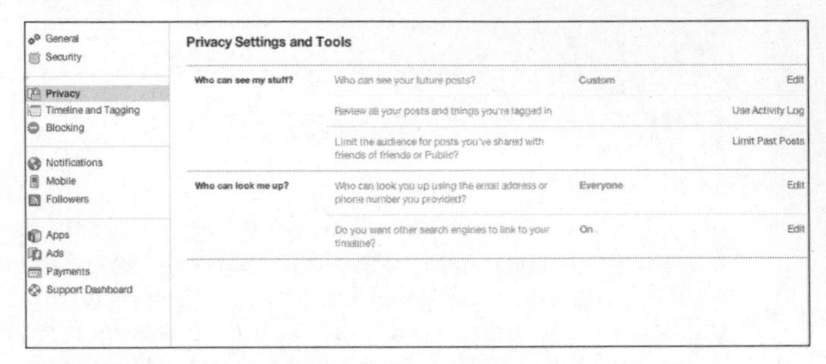

Figure 3-4: Start here to set privacy options.

Privacy section

The Privacy section of the Settings page (refer to Figure 3-4) has two sections: Who Can See My Stuff? and Who Can Look Me Up?

Who can see my stuff?

The Who Can See My Stuff section should look familiar if you read the section on privacy shortcuts. Two of the three settings are redundant with the Privacy Shortcuts menu:

- **Who can see your future posts?** This setting shows you your current setting for when you create posts. This is who can see all your future posts (unless you change it). To change this setting, click the Edit link on the right side of the page. A sample share menu appears where you can choose a new privacy setting.
- **Review all your posts and things you're tagged in.** This setting provides a link to Activity Log, a granular list of everything you've done on Facebook. I cover how to use Activity Log in the "Privacy Tools" section later in this chapter.
- **Limit the audience for posts you've shared with Friends of Friends or Public.** This setting is needed only if you shared posts with Everyone or with Friends of Friends. If you've shared only with Friends (or an even smaller subset of people), this setting won't change anything. Use it to change the privacy settings of all items that were previously public to be visible only to Friends.

This setting might be useful if, for example, you're job hunting and don't want potential employers to find your public posts about the most recent election. Once you make this change, it can't be undone. In other words, those posts will always be visible only to friends unless you go back and individually make them public.

To use this setting, click the Limit Past Posts link on the right side of the page, and then click the Limit Old Posts button that appears.

Who can look me up?

The Who Can Look Me Up? section concerns how people can find you on Facebook. When you signed up for Facebook, you entered an e-mail address and possibly a phone number. The first setting asks if people who search by that information will be able to find you. If you're someone who has a slightly different name than your real name on your Timeline (for example, if I were to go by Carolyn EA on Facebook rather than my actual name, Carolyn Abram), I recommend leaving this setting set to Everyone. Limiting it limits your potential friends' ability to find you.

To change this setting, click Edit on the right side of the page and use the Privacy menu to select whether Everyone, Friends of Friends, or only Friends can search for you by e-mail or phone number.

The second setting here concerns search engine indexing. Search engines like Google use web crawlers to create indexes they can search to provide results to users. So when someone searches for your name on Google, a link to your Facebook Timeline appears by default unless you deselect this setting.

To change this setting, click edit on the right side of the page and deselect the check box labeled Let Other Search Engines Link to Your Timeline. Click Confirm in the pop-up window that appears.

Even if you deselect the search engine indexing check box, people will still be able to search for you by name on Facebook itself. With the exception of someone you have blocked, people will always be able to search for you and get to your Timeline from Facebook Search.

Timeline and tagging section

The Timeline, as I describe in Chapter 2, is basically where you collect all your stuff on Facebook. That means photos, posts, posts friends have left you, application activity, and so on. Your Timeline allows you to look through your history and represent yourself to your friends.

Tags on Facebook are a way of labeling people in your content. For example, when uploading a photo, you can tag a specific friend in it. That tag becomes information that others can see as well as a link back to your friend's Timeline. In addition, from your friend's Timeline, people can get to that photo to see her smiling face. You can tag people and pages in status updates, photos, notes, check-ins at various places, comments, and any other type of post. And just like you can tag friends, friends can tag you in their photos and posts.

This section of the settings page allows you to control settings related to people interacting with you on your Timeline and tagging you in posts. For controlling the privacy on things you add to your Timeline, you use the Privacy menu in the Share box. The Timeline and Tagging Settings section is shown in Figure 3-5.

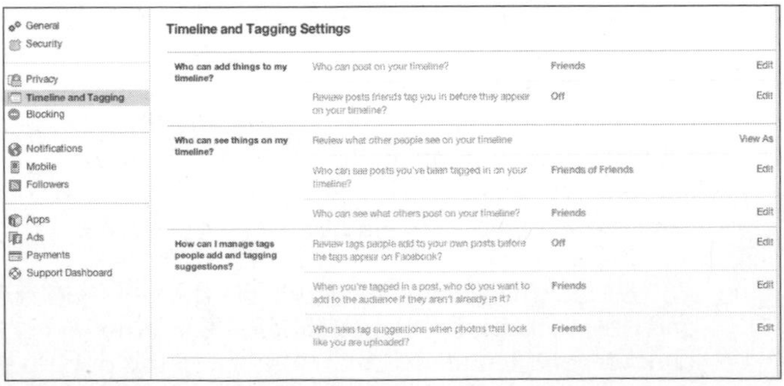

Figure 3-5: Edit your settings for tags.

Who can add things to my timeline?

The Who Can Add Things to My Timeline section focuses on other people adding things like photos, posts, or tags to your Timeline:

- **Who can post on your Timeline?** In addition to being a place where you add posts, your Timeline is a place where your friends can leave you messages or posts. If you don't want your friends leaving these sorts of public messages (if you're using Facebook for professional or networking reasons, for example), set this to Only Me.

  By default, only friends can post on your Timeline. This setting means no one can post to your Timeline except you.

  To change this setting, click Edit on the right side of the setting and use the drop-down menu that appears to select Only Me.

- **Review posts friends tag you in before they appear on your Timeline.** Timeline Review allows you to review the tags people have added of you before they're displayed on your Timeline. In other words, if I tag you in a photo, that photo won't appear on your Timeline until you log in to Facebook and approve the tag.

  To change this setting, click Edit on the right side of the setting and use the drop-down menu that appears to toggle between Enabled and Disabled. By default, tags of you are automatically approved, and this setting is set to Disabled.

Who can see things on my timeline?

Adding things to your Timeline, which the preceding settings control, is not the same as simply *looking* at your Timeline, which the settings in the Who Can See Things on My Timeline section control. Three settings here concern what people see when they look at your profile:

- **Review what other people see on your Timeline.** This setting is actually a link to the View As privacy tool (which I cover in detail in the "Privacy Tools" section later in this chapter). The View As tool allows you to look at your Timeline as though you're someone else, thus double-checking that your privacy settings are actually working.
- **Who can see posts in which you've been tagged on your Timeline?** After you've approved tags (or if you leave Timeline Review off), you can still decide who can see the content in which you're tagged on your Timeline.

In other words, if your friend tags you in a photo, you can control who sees that photo on *your* Timeline. The idea behind this setting is that, although you will never post anything embarrassing to your Timeline, a friend might do so. Making sure that not everyone can see that post cuts down on any awkwardness.

To change this setting, click the Edit link and choose who can see this information.

- **Who can see what others post on your Timeline?** Another way to control the "embarrassing friend on your Timeline" problem is to limit who can see the posts your friends leave. To change this setting, click the Edit link and choose who can see these posts.

How Can I Manage Tags People Add and Tagging Suggestions?

Although tagging has been mentioned in many of these Timeline settings, the settings in the How Can I Manage Tags People Add and Tagging Suggestions? section refer to specific cases of tagging:

- **Review tags people add to your own posts before the tags appear on Facebook.** This setting controls tags that your friends add to content you've uploaded. For example, if I upload a photo of 20 people to Facebook and don't tag anyone in it, my friends might choose to add tags. This setting lets me choose to review the tags my friends add before the tag is visible to other people. To change this setting, click Edit and choose whether Tag Review is Enabled or Disabled (the default).
- **When you're tagged in a post, whom do you want to add to the audience if they aren't already in it?** This setting is a little complicated. Say that I'm friends with Eric and Dave, but Eric is not friends with Dave. Now say that Eric adds a photo of me (meaning he has tagged me in it), and his privacy settings share that photo with his friends. Because Dave and Eric aren't friends, Dave cannot see that photo unless this setting allows my friends to be added to the audience of that photo.

  To change this setting, click Edit and choose who is added to the audience of a post you're tagged in. By default, this setting adds your friends to the audience of a post you're tagged in.

- **Who sees tag suggestions when photos that look like you are uploaded?** Facebook employs some facial recognition software to help people tag photos. So if a friend is uploading 50 photos and you appear in 30 of them, Facebook might recognize your face and suggest to your friend that you be tagged in those 30 photos. This feature saves your friend time while he's adding photos and encourages people to add more tags to Facebook. You can choose not to appear in the suggestions Facebook gives your friends by disabling this setting. To change this setting, click Edit and choose whether Friends or No One will see tag suggestions.

Blocking section

Most of your privacy settings are preventative measures for making yourself comfortable on Facebook. Blocklists are usually more reactive. If someone does something on Facebook that bothers you, you may choose to block him or block certain actions he takes. The Blocking section of the Settings page is shown in Figure 3-6. You can manage five blocklists here: Restricted List, Block Users, Block App Invites, Block Event Invites, and Block Apps.

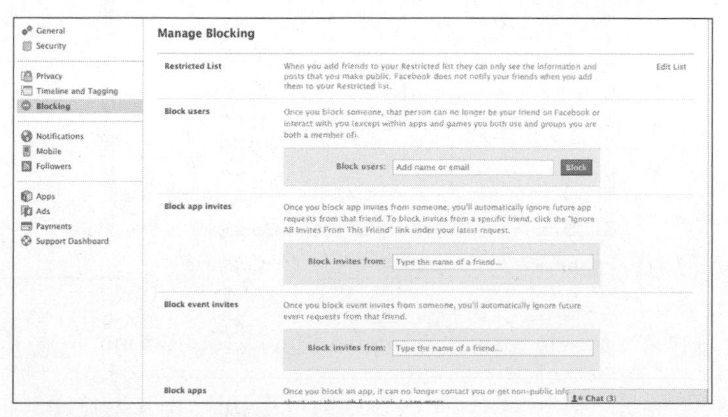

Figure 3-6: Edit your blocklists here.

Restricted List

The Restricted List is a list you can create that's not quite as serious as blocking someone outright but is slightly more serious than simply adding the person to your Acquaintances list. For example, say that you receive Friend Requests from Veronica and Logan. You accept the Friend Requests and add Veronica to the Acquaintances list and Logan to the Restricted list. Whenever you add a post that is visible to Everyone, both can see it. When you add a post that is visible to Friends Except Acquaintances, neither can see it. However, when you add a post that is visible to Friends, Veronica will be able to see it, but Logan won't be able to. Make sense?

To add someone to this list, click Edit List on the right side of the page. A pop-up window appears, as shown in Figure 3-7. If you've already added people to this list, they appear here, and you can remove them from the list by hovering your cursor over their pictures and clicking the x that appears in the right corner of the photos.

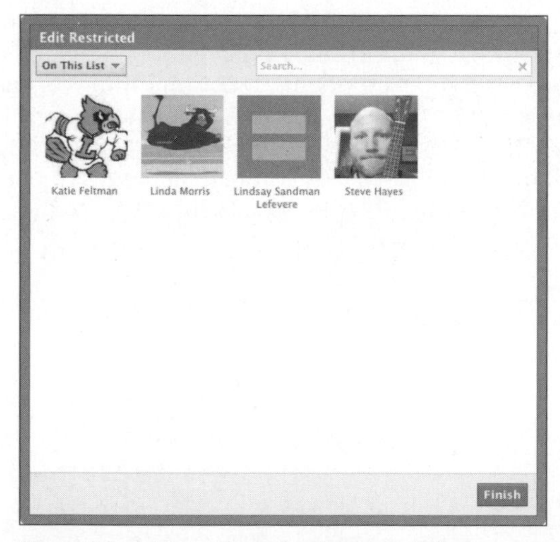

Figure 3-7: Add people to the Restricted List.

To add people to the list, follow these steps:

1. **Click the On This List button, in the top left, and then click Friends.**

   You see an alphabetical grid of all your friends.

2. **Add friends to the Restricted List by clicking their pictures or by searching for them by name in the upper-right corner and then clicking their pictures.**

3. **When you're done, click the Finish button.**

Block Users

Blocking someone is the strongest way to distance yourself from someone else on Facebook. For the most part, if you add someone to your Block list, he can't see any traces of you on Facebook. You won't show up in his News Feed; if he looks at a photo in which you're tagged, he may see you in the photo (that's unavoidable), but he won't see that your name has been tagged. When you write on other people's Timelines, your posts are hidden from him. Here are a few key things to remember about blocking:

- **Blocking is almost entirely reciprocal.** If you block someone, she is just as invisible to you as you are to her. So you can't access her Timeline, nor can you see anything about her anywhere on the site. The only difference is that if you blocked the relationship, you're the only one who can unblock it.
- **People you block are not notified that you blocked them.** Nor are they notified if you unblock them. If they are savvy Facebook users, they may notice your suspicious absence, but Facebook never tells them that they have been blocked by you.
- **You can block people who are your friends or who are not your friends.** If you are friends with someone and then you block her, Facebook also removes the friendship. If you unblock her later, you will need to re-friend her.

Blocking on Facebook doesn't necessarily extend to apps and games you use on Facebook and around the Internet. Contact the developers of the apps you use to learn how to block people within games and apps.

To add people to your blocklist, simply enter their names or e-mail addresses into the boxes provided. Then click the Block button, and you will see their names in a list. To remove the block, click the Unblock link next to their names.

Block App Invites

An *application* is a term used to describe pieces of software that use Facebook data, even when those applications weren't built by Facebook. As friends use apps and games, they may send you an invite to join them. This is all well and good until you find that certain people send you wayyyy too many invites. Rather than unfriend or block the overly friendly person, you can simply block invitations. This option still allows you to interact with your friend in every other way, but you won't receive application invites from him or her.

To block invites from a specific person, just type the person's name in the Block Invites From box, and click Enter when you're done. That person's name then appears on the list below the text box. To remove the block, click Unblock next to that name.

Block Event Invites

Similar to App Invites, you may have friends who are big planners and love to invite all their friends to their events. These may be events that you have no chance of attending because they're taking place across the country. Your friend is cool, but his endless unnecessary invitations are not. Instead of getting rid of your friend, you can get rid of the invitations by entering his name here.

To block event invites from specific people, just type their names in the Block Invites From box. Click Enter when you're done. Their names then appear on the list below the text box. To remove the block, click Unblock next to their names.

Block Apps

Occasionally, an app behaves badly once you start using it. By "behaves badly," I mean things like spamming your friends or using your information in ways that make you uncomfortable. If an app is doing so, you can block it to prevent it from contacting you through Facebook and getting updated Facebook information about you.

To block an app, type its name in the Block Apps text field and press Enter. The name of the app appears on the list below the text box. To remove the block, click Unblock next to its name.

Apps section

An *app* is a term used to describe pieces of software that use Facebook data, even when those applications weren't built by Facebook. You may use apps as games, websites, and useful tools, all of which make use of the data you already share on Facebook. To make it easier to get people using these applications, the data is imported from Facebook. I cover the specifics on using applications in Chapter 8. For now, keep in mind that the apps you see on this page are those you chose to interact with. You won't see random applications appear here without you giving them some permissions first.

The Apps section, shown in Figure 3-8, is where you edit how apps, games, and websites interact with your Timeline.

Figure 3-8: App settings.

Apps You Use

The Apps You Use section shows all the apps you've used, most recent first. Apps you use require direct permission from you to begin accessing your data and posting to your Timeline. Next to each app's name in this list is the audience that can see that app on your Timeline. Click the Edit link across from an app to see a menu of settings (see Figure 3-9).

Just above the list of apps is a small setting that asks whether you want to Use Apps, Plugins, Games, and Websites on Facebook and Elsewhere. By default, this setting is On. If you don't want to use any applications ever, you can turn it off. I don't recommend turning it off because apps can be fun and useful, both on Facebook and across the web.

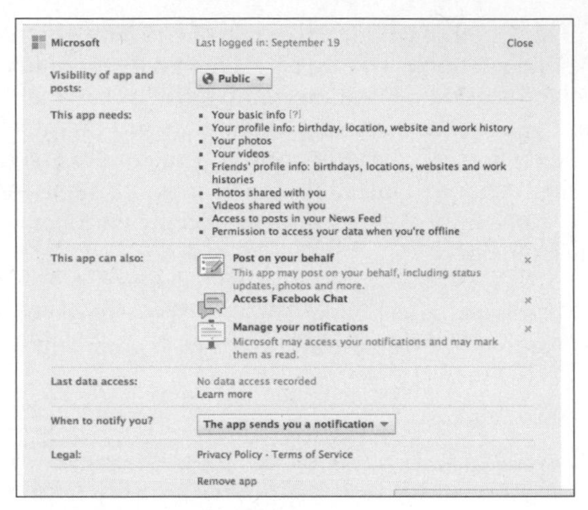

Figure 3-9: Edit App settings here.

Each app has several sections of information. Some sections have options you can change, and others are merely informative:

- **Last Logged In:** This area lists the last time you logged into the app and used it.
- **Visibility of App:** The Privacy menu here has the same options as any other Privacy menu. You can choose who can see your activity in an app. For example, I keep my Kickstarter app visible to friends because I like them to know what projects I'm supporting. I make my Hulu app visible to Only Me because I'm ashamed of how much reality television I watch.
- **This App Needs:** This list of information shows you what Timeline information the app requires to function. For example, the Fandango app requires my likes and my friends' likes. Most likely, it uses this information to recommend movies I might like to see. If you ever see a piece of information on this list that doesn't make sense, it might be a hint that the app isn't reputable. You could then choose to remove or block the app.
- **This App Can Also:** This section, which might not be present for all apps, reflects any special permissions you may have granted to an app. Special permissions are things like access to Facebook Chat or adding posts on your behalf. You can remove a permission by clicking the x next to it in this section.

Certain permissions are required by apps if you want to use them. That means you can't take the permission away unless you choose to remove the app entirely.

- **Last Data Access:** This area shows the last piece of information the app accessed about you and when it accessed that info.
- **When to Notify You?** Apps may send you notifications about activity your friends have taken or other info you might want to know. You can choose to let applications send you notifications whenever it wants or never.
- **Legal:** These links take you to the app's Privacy Policy and Terms of Service.
- **Remove App:** At the bottom of the section is a link you can click to remove an app. Removing an app revokes the permissions you have given it and the app won't be able to access your private information going forward.

Apps Others Use

Even if you don't use applications, your friends might. Similar to the way that you might not add photos to Facebook but your friends might add and tag photos of you, your friends might also pass on information about you to applications. You can restrict what applications can see by using the check boxes pictured in Figure 3-10.

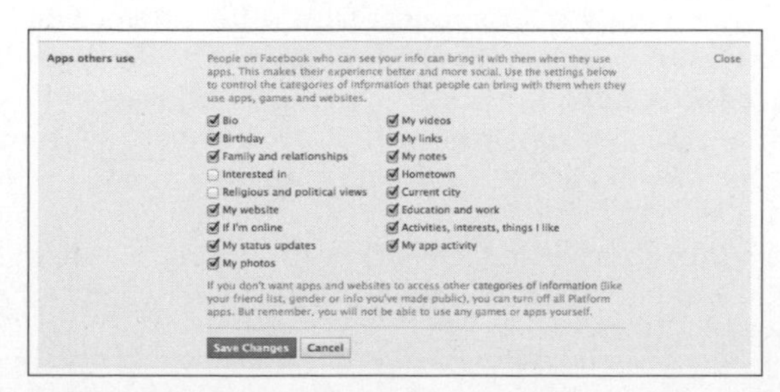

Figure 3-10: What can your friends share with apps and games?

Instant Personalization

Instant Personalization is a Facebook feature that lets certain Facebook partners access your public Facebook information using browser information, as opposed to using the permission dialog boxes that most apps use before they get access to any information. These partners are websites like Bing,

Yelp, and Pandora. You can turn off Instant Personalization by clicking Edit on the right side of the page and deselecting the Enable Instant Personalization on Partner Websites check box. You may be presented with a pop-up window with a video first. You can watch the video or just close the window to continue on to change your setting.

Old Versions of Facebook for Mobile

If you've never used Facebook on a mobile phone or are certain you're using the most recent Facebook app on an iPhone or Android phone, this setting doesn't apply to you. But if you're using a version of Facebook for Mobile that doesn't allow you to change your privacy for each post you create, you can use this setting to control who sees posts you make from your phone. Click Edit on the right side of the page and use the Privacy menu that appears to make your selection.

Ads section

The Ads section of the settings page has two settings, both of which require a lot of explanation. The first setting, called Third Party Sites, is perhaps the most confusing because it's a setting that does nothing. Fundamentally, it asks if Facebook can share your information with other sites. However, Facebook currently doesn't share information with other sites.

When Facebook does show ads on other sites (which it does), your data remains on Facebook's servers and doesn't get shared with anyone else. So when Facebook asks if you want to share this information with your friends or with no one, it applies only if Facebook changes its policy.

To change this setting, click Edit on the right side of the page and use the drop-down menu to toggle between Only My Friends and No One.

The second setting is called Ads & Friends. Facebook pays its bills not by charging you money but by showing you ads and charging advertisers for that privilege. Facebook differentiates its ads from other ads on the Internet by pointing out that their ads are "social." In other words, if my friend likes something, there's a good chance I will like it, too. So in its ads, whenever possible, Facebook includes social information. You can see an example of this in Figure 3-11.

Figure 3-11: Two ads — one doesn't have social information and one does.

I'm comfortable with my friends seeing things that I've liked, public events I've attended, or places I've checked in paired with an ad for that thing, event, or place. If you aren't comfortable with this, you can prevent it from happening.

To prevent your friends from seeing any information about you next to an advertisement, click Edit on the right side of the page. Use the drop-down menu that appears (below all the text) to toggle between Only My Friends and No One. Click Save Changes when you're done.

Even if you don't change this setting, only your friends ever see information about you next to ads. If we're not friends, you'll never see a notice that "Carolyn Abram likes this movie" next to an advertisement for a popular film.

Timeline Privacy

In addition to the content you post — which was covered earlier in the "Privacy When Sharing" section — you can control the information that you've entered in the About and Interests sections of your Timeline. This information, such as where you went to school or your relationship status, changes infrequently, if ever.

All about privacy

You can edit the privacy for your content in the About and Interests section in the same place you edit the information itself. To get there, go to your Timeline and click the Update Info button in the bottom-right corner of your cover photo.

The About page has several sections, each representing a different information category. So, for example, all your work and education information appears in the Work and Education section. Click the Edit button in the upper-right corner of a section to access additional editing options for that category. Next to each piece of information, a privacy icon appears signifying who can see that piece of information. By default, most of this information is set to Public and visible to Everyone, although contact information is visible only to Friends by default.

Figure 3-12 shows me editing the privacy for a piece of information — in this case, my current city in the Living section of my About page. Clicking the privacy icon to the right of the field displays the Audience Selector. When you've finished changing your settings for any particular category, remember to click Save wherever it appears.

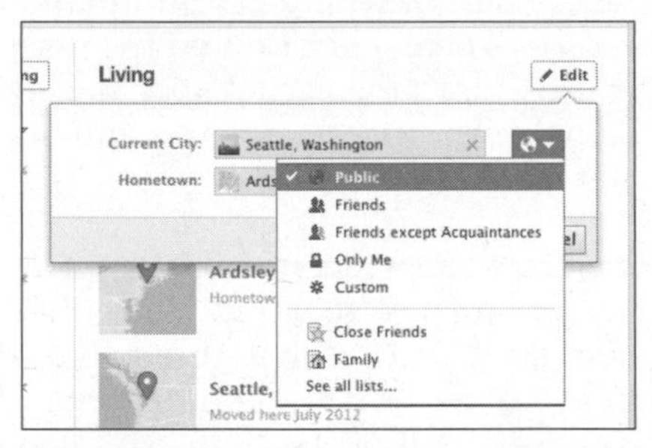

Figure 3-12: Edit privacy for every piece of information on your Timeline.

Timeline information is one of the places where the Only Me setting might come in handy. For example, lots of people don't like sharing their birthdays on Facebook, but Facebook requires you to enter a birthday when you sign up. By making it visible only to you, you hide your birthday from everyone.

Click Save Changes when you're done editing privacy settings. Otherwise, the new settings won't stick.

Interested in privacy

If you're looking at your About page and continue scrolling down past all the information sections, you come to the Interest sections. Interests are sorted into categories like Movies, Music, and Books. For your TV Shows section, for example, you can add TV shows that you've watched, TV shows that you want to watch, and TV shows that you like. Each time you add a TV show to the list of shows you've watched or want to watch, you can also control who sees that you've added that particular show to that list. Figure 3-13 shows me editing who can see that I've watched the BBC show *Sherlock*. I opened this Privacy menu by clicking the privacy icon below the image representing the show.

Figure 3-13: Selecting who can see what I've watched.

I can also control who can see what TV shows I like. Unlike the Watched and Want to Watch sections, where I can edit this individually, I decide who can see *all* the shows I've liked. To edit who can see what you've liked, follow these steps:

1. **Make sure you're looking at the correct section on your screen.**

   In this case, I'm looking at the TV Shows box.

2. **Click the pencil icon in the upper-right corner of the box.**

   A menu of options related to this section appears.

3. **Click Edit Privacy.**

   A pop-up window opens.

4. **In the section of the box labeled Likes, click the Privacy menu.**

   This opens the Privacy menu with familiar options: Public, Friends, Friends Except Acquaintances, Only Me, Custom, or Lists.

5. **Choose whom you want to see the TV shows you have liked.**

6. **Click Close to save the changes.**

Privacy Tools

Okay, that was a lot. A lot of settings, a lot of information. What if you don't want to worry about these small settings and who tagged what when? What if you just want to make sure that your Timeline looks the way you want to your friends and that people who aren't your friends can't see anything you don't want them to see? Well, the good news is that the View As tool allows you to do just that, and the Activity Log tool allows you to keep track of everything that's been happening recently and to make any needed adjustments without trying to figure out which setting needs to be changed.

View As

You can get to the View As tool from the Privacy Shortcuts menu. Click the lock icon next to your name in the left sidebar to open the menu up. In the Who Can See My Stuff? section, click the link to View As.

Clicking that link brings you to your Timeline, but the view is not how you usually see your Timeline. The black bar running across the top of the page lets you know that you're currently viewing your Timeline as someone who is not your friend (also known as everyone in the Public bucket of people). You can click through to the various sections of your Timeline.

Note that no matter how much you've hidden your information and posts, everyone can see your cover photo and profile picture, gender, current city, and Friend List. Anything else the public can see can be hidden, if you so choose.

In the black bar on top of this view of your Timeline is a white bold link labeled View as Specific Person. If you want to check on, for example, what acquaintances or people you've added to your Restricted list can see, click this link and enter a friend's name in the text box that appears. If you're surprised by what that friend can see, you can go change the privacy on any content you don't want her to see. (If you've forgotten how to change the privacy on a post, head back up to the "Privacy When Sharing" section.)

I'm having a privacy freakout!

I cannot tell you how many times I've received a frantic e-mail from a family member or friend saying something like, "Oh my gosh, my friend just told me that his friend was able to see some photos that I thought only my friends could see and now I'm freaking out that everyone can see everything. Do you know what to do?"

The first step is to take a deep breath. After that, the next best thing to do is to go to the Privacy Shortcuts menu and click the View As tool. You can then click around your Timeline as though you're someone who isn't your friend. If you think that person is seeing too much, I recommend using the Limit the Audience for Past Posts setting on the Privacy section of the Settings page. This pretty much changes anything that used to be visible to more than just friends to be visible only to Friends. After you do that, usually you can begin the process of adjusting your settings so that, going forward, you won't have any more freakouts.

Activity Log

As you've probably noticed, a lot happens on Facebook. You take all sorts of actions: liking, commenting, posting, and so on. And people take all sorts of actions that affect you: writing on your Timeline, tagging you in photos, and inviting you to join groups. If you want to know, line by line, everything that could possibly be seen about you by someone on Facebook, Activity Log is for you.

You can get to Activity Log from a few places. You can get there from the Privacy Shortcuts menu or from your own Timeline. On your Timeline, simply click the Activity Log button, located under the right corner of your cover photo. This takes you to Activity Log (see Figure 3-14).

When you're looking at Activity Log, note the menu on the left for viewing only certain types of posts. For example, you can choose to view all the posts you've been tagged in, or all the photo posts, or all the app-related posts.

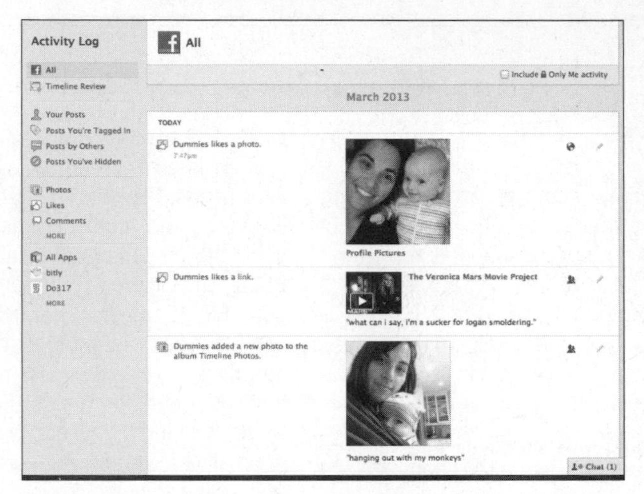

Figure 3-14: Here's everything you've done on Facebook recently.

When you're looking at an individual line item, you see several columns of information. First is an icon and sentence explaining what you did (or what a friend did). This might be something like "Carolyn wrote on Dana's Timeline" or "Carolyn was tagged in Dana's photo." Then there is a preview of that post, photo, comment, or whatever it is related to. For example, if you commented on a photo, the preview will show you that photo and the comment that you made.

To the right of the preview is an icon representing who can see that item. Hover your cursor over the icon to see text explaining who can see it. This might be the usual privacy options, or it might be members of a group you belong to, or in the case of a post to a friend's Timeline, it will be that person's friends. For posts that you create, you can change the audience by clicking the icon, which opens the Privacy menu.

However, you'll find that you can't change the privacy on lots of content. For example, a comment on someone else's post isn't something you can change the audience for. If you realize a comment you made or something you liked is visible to more people than you'd want, your only option is to delete that content.

You can delete content using the final icon to the right side of each item in Activity Log. This little pencil icon can be found all over the site and generally indicates that you can edit something.

When you hover your cursor over the icon here, it explains that the item is allowed on Timeline. This means that people may see that item — possibly as its own post, as a summarized item in recent activity, or in an app box — when they visit your Timeline. Clicking the Edit button reveals a menu of options for changing whether something appears on Timeline. For some items, such as likes or comments, the only option is to unlike the content or delete the comment. For others, like posts you've made or posts you've been tagged in, there are more options that allow you to hide something from the Timeline or edit it on your Timeline (these are the same options that appear when you go to edit or highlight something on your Timeline).

When I say something is visible on Timeline, I also mean that your friends might see that item in their News Feed.

I find Activity Log useful in that it helps me understand all the ways I participate on Facebook and all the things my friends might see about me and my life. But I've found that I don't change the privacy or the Timeline settings on items here all that often.

Remembering That It Takes a Village to Raise a Facebook

Another way in which you (and every member of Facebook) contribute to keeping Facebook a safe, clean place is in the reports that you submit about spam, harassment, inappropriate content, and fake Timelines. Almost every piece of content on Facebook can be reported. Sometimes you may need to click an Options link to find the report link.

Figure 3-15 shows an example of someone reporting an inappropriate photo.

Figure 3-15: Reporting inappropriate content.

The various reporting options that you see may vary, depending on what you're reporting (a group as opposed to a photo, for example). These reports are submitted to the Facebook User Operations team. The team then investigates and takes down inappropriate photos, disables fake accounts, and generally strives to keep Facebook clean, safe, and inoffensive.

When you see content that you don't like — for example, an offensive group name or a vulgar Timeline — don't hesitate to report it. With the entire Facebook population working to keep Facebook free of badness, you wind up with a pretty awesome community.

After you report something, Facebook's User Operations team evaluates it in terms of violating Facebook's Statement of Rights and Responsibilities. This means that pornography gets taken down, fake Timelines are disabled, and people who send spam may receive a warning or even have their account disabled. However, sometimes something that you report may be offensive to you but doesn't violate the Statement of Rights and Responsibilities and, therefore, will remain on Facebook. Due to privacy restrictions, User Operations may not always notify you about actions taken as a result of your support, but rest assured that the team handles every report.

The best way to protect yourself from phishing is to get used to the times and places Facebook asks for your password. If you just clicked a link in Facebook and suddenly a blue screen asks for your information, be suspicious! Similarly, remember that Facebook will never ask you to e-mail it your password. If you receive an e-mail asking for something like that, report it as spam immediately.

If you want to stay up-to-date with the latest scams on Facebook, or want more information about protecting yourself, you can like Facebook's Security Page at `www.facebook.com/security`. This link provides you with ongoing information about safety and security on Facebook.

Chapter 4

Finding Facebook Friends

In This Chapter

- Understanding what *friending* someone means
- Finding friends on Facebook in various ways
- Organizing and managing your Friend Lists

Most of Facebook's functionality is built around the premise that you have a certain amount of information that you want your friends to see. If you don't have friends who are seeing your posts and viewing your photos, what's the point in sharing them?

On Facebook, the bulk of friendships are *reciprocal,* which means if you add someone as a friend, he or she has to confirm the friendship before it appears on both Timelines. If someone adds you as a friend, you can choose between Confirm and Not Now. If you confirm the friend, *Congrats!* You have a new friend! And if you ignore the friend, the other person won't be informed.

What Is a Facebook Friend?

In many ways, a *Facebook friend* is the same as a real-life friend. These are the people you hang out with, keep in touch with, care about, and want to publicly acknowledge as friends. However, friendship has lots of shades — think of the differences between acquaintances, a friend from work, an activity buddy, and best friends. Facebook gives you a few tools for negotiating these levels of friendship, which I cover later in the chapter. But by default, most friendships are lumped into a blanket category of "friend."

Here are the basics of what it means to be friends with someone on Facebook:

- **They can see all the stuff on your Timeline (like your posts and other information) that you have set to be visible to Friends.**

  Remember, this is what happens by default. You can control which friends can see which posts more by using privacy options (see Chapter 3), and Friend Lists, which I go over later in this chapter.

- **They see new posts you create in their News Feeds on their Home pages.**

  The information your friends see in their News Feeds depends on the audience you've chosen to share each post with and possibly on your friends' News Feed settings.

- **You can see their posts and other information on their Timelines.**

  What you see depends on their privacy settings. In general, you'll be able to see more as a friend than you did before you became friends.

- **You see new posts from them in your News Feed on your Home page.**

  What you see depends on your friends' sharing settings. You can control whose posts you see in your News Feed by managing your own News Feed settings and preferences, as you discover later in the chapter.

- **You'll be listed as friends on one another's Timeline.**

  This small detail is important in understanding the difference between becoming friends with someone and simply subscribing to someone's posts. Lots of people, especially public figures or people who have a business of some sort, allow you to subscribe to their posts without becoming friends. You see their posts on your Home page, but they won't see your posts unless they choose to subscribe to you.

Adding Friends

Friending is the act of adding someone as a friend. You may overhear people use this casually in conversation: "Oh, you won't believe who finally friended me!" And now you, too, will be friending people.

Sending Friend Requests

Now that you know what a friend is, it's time to send some requests, and maybe even accept some pending ones. For this example, I searched for the Timeline of Dummies Man using the Search box in the blue bar on top. I cover using Search to find friends later in this chapter; for now just remember that as you type, Facebook tries to autocomplete what you're looking for, meaning search results will appear below the Search box as you type, as shown in Figure 4-1.

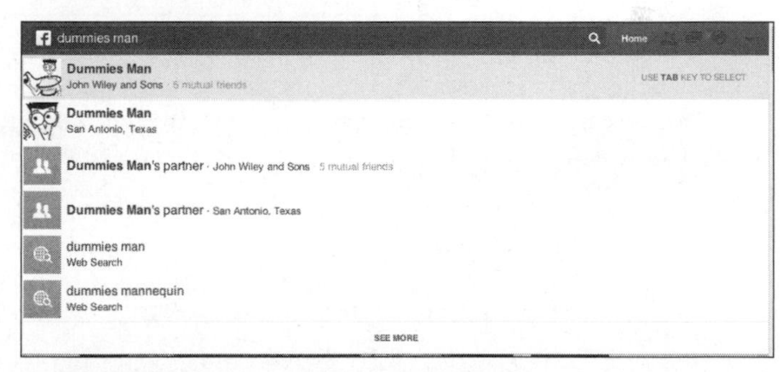

Figure 4-1: The search results for Dummies Man.

When you see the person you think you want to add, click her face; this takes you to her Timeline. At the bottom-right corner of her cover photo, click the Add Friend button (see Figure 4-2) to send a Friend Request. When she accepts the request, you'll become friends.

Figure 4-2: A Timeline before I become a friend.

You won't be friends with someone until she confirms your Friend Request. After she confirms, you're notified by a red flag above the notifications icon in the blue bar on top.

So what does your potential friend see after you send a request? That is a brilliant segue into the next topic, accepting Friend Requests.

Accepting Friend Requests

When you receive a new request, a little red flag appears over the Friends icon in the big blue bar on top of each page (see Figure 4-3). You may also be notified in your e-mail or on your phone. The number in the red flag indicates how many Friend Requests are waiting for you.

Figure 4-3: Someone wants to be your friend!

Clicking the Friends icon opens the Friend Requests menu, as shown in Figure 4-4. To accept the Friend Request, click the Confirm button. You now have a friend. To reject the request, click Not Now.

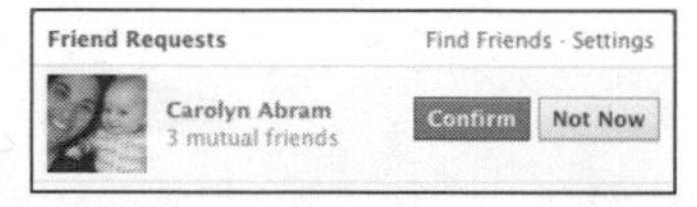

Figure 4-4: Click Confirm or Not Now.

When you click Not Now, Facebook may ask you whether you know that person outside Facebook. In other words, is this a Friend Request from someone you know or someone you don't know? If you click No, Facebook prevents that person from friending you again. If you click Yes, Facebook hides the request. To get back to hidden Friend Requests, open the Friend Request menu and choose See All. You see a page displaying all outstanding requests, including hidden ones. You can then confirm or permanently delete a request.

You can access hidden requests also by going to the Timeline of the person who sent the request. Click the Friend Request button to become official Facebook friends.

Some people worry about clicking that Not Now button. If you're not sure what you want to do, you can always leave the request untouched. But never hesitate to click Not Now for someone you just don't want to be friends with. Facebook won't notify her that you ignored her request.

Choosing your friends wisely

Generally, you send Friend Requests to and confirm Friend Requests from only people you know. If you don't know them, click Not Now. Accepting a Friend Request from people you don't know tends to ruin the Facebook experience by putting random content in your News Feed and exposing your content to people you don't know.

For people you don't know personally but find interesting (such as a celebrity or a public figure), you may be able to subscribe to their posts without becoming friends (see the "Following people" section near the end of this chapter).

Another common misperception about Facebook is that it's all about the race to get the most friends. This is wrong. Between the News Feed and privacy implications of friendship, aim to keep your Friend List to the people you care about.

As you change jobs or cities or start a new hobby, you add more friends, but that doesn't displace the fact that you care about friends from your past. The Friend List management tools aim to help you keep track of the people you care about most, and not get distracted by more distant friends.

Finding Friends on Facebook

How do you get to the people you want to be your friends? Facebook is big, and if you're looking for your friend John, you may need to provide more detail. Facebook has a couple of tools that show you people you may know and want as your friends, as well as a normal search-by-name functionality for finding specific people.

Using the Friend Finder

The *Friend Finder* tool matches e-mail addresses in your e-mail address book to people's Timelines on Facebook. With your permission, Friend Finder also invites people who don't have a Facebook account but whose e-mail addresses match those in your address book to join Facebook. Sending invites this way automatically sends Friend Requests to those people.

To use Friend Finder, you need to give Facebook your e-mail address and e-mail password. Facebook doesn't store this information but does use it to retrieve your contacts list once. The following steps make several assumptions — namely, that you use web-based e-mail (such as Hotmail, Gmail, or Yahoo! Mail), that you haven't used Friend Finder recently, and that the address book for the e-mail contains a bunch of your friends. I cover other options, such as a client-based address book, later in the chapter.

Here's how to use Friend Finder:

1. **Click the Friends icon on the big blue bar on top.**

   The Friend Request menu opens.

2. **Click the Find Friends link in the menu.**

   Figure 4-5 shows the Friend Finder. Below it, you may also see a list of People You May Know (not shown in figure), which I cover later in this chapter.

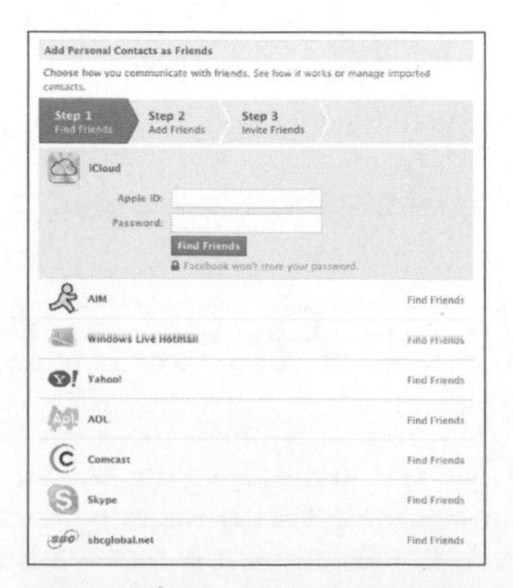

Figure 4-5: An unfilled Friend Finder.

3. **Select the e-mail or instant message service you use.**

   This service may be Windows Live Hotmail, AOL, iCloud, or any number of other e-mail services.

4. **Enter your e-mail address in the Your Email field.**

5. **Enter your e-mail password (not your Facebook password) in the Email Password box and then click Find Friends.**

   These instructions are meant for first-time users of the Friend Finder. If you've used it before, or if you're currently logged in to your webmail client, you may see some fields prefilled or additional pop-up prompts asking you for your permission to send information to Facebook. Don't worry if what you see on the screen doesn't match some of the figures.

   If Facebook finds matches with the e-mails in your address book, you see a page similar to Figure 4-6. (If Facebook doesn't find any friends, go to Step 7.)

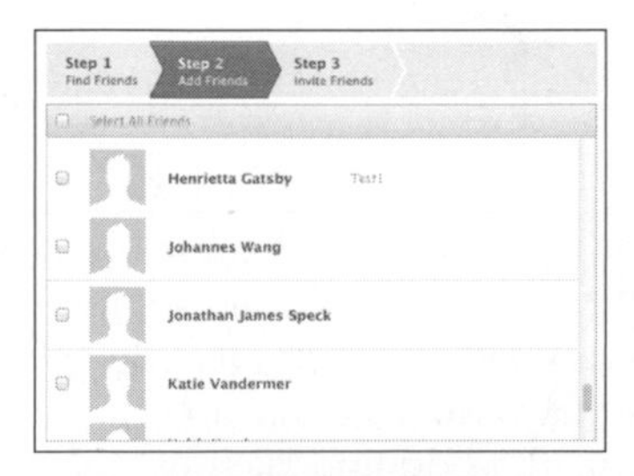

Figure 4-6: The friend selector portion of Friend Finder.

6. **Decide whether to**

   - *Add everyone as a friend.* Make sure the Select All Friends check box (in the grey bar above the results) is selected, and then click the Add Friends button.
   - *Not friend anyone.* Make sure the Select All Friends check box is deselected, and then click Skip.
   - *Add specific people as friends.* Click the faces or select the check boxes to the left of the names of people you want to be friends with, and then click Add Friends.

Everyone you select receives a Friend Request.

After you click either Add Friends or Skip, you land on the Invite Friends portion of Friend Finder. Here you find a list of contact names and e-mail addresses. These e-mails or phone numbers are those that don't have matches on Facebook.

7. **(Optional) Invite people to join Facebook and become your friends.**

   Similar to adding friends, you can

   - *Invite all these contacts.* Make sure the Select All/None box is selected and click Send Invites.
   - *Invite none of these contacts.* Make sure the Select All/None box is deselected and click Skip.
   - *Invite some of these contacts.* Select the Invite Some Friends option and then select the check box to the left of each e-mail address that you want to invite to join Facebook.

   After you make your selections, click Send Invites or Invite to Join. If you don't want to send any invitations, click Skip.

After taking all these steps, I hope you manage to send at least a few Friend Requests. Don't be shy about adding people you know and want to keep up with; it's not considered rude to add people as your friends. Your friends need to confirm your requests before you officially become friends on Facebook, so you may not be able to see your friends' Timelines until those confirmations happen.

If the experience yielded nothing — no friends you wanted to add, no contacts you wanted to invite — you have a few options. You can go through these steps again with different e-mail addresses. If that's not the problem, you have more ways to use Friend Finder.

Import an address book

If you're someone who uses a *desktop e-mail client* — a program on your local computer that manages your e-mail (such as Microsoft Outlook), create a file of your contacts and import it so that Facebook can check it for friend matches.

The way to create your contact file depends on which e-mail client you use. Here's how to get the right instructions:

1. **From the Friend Finder, select the Other Tools option.**
2. **Click Upload Contact File, the first blue link.**

   If you're using a Mac, you may see a blue Find My Mac Address Book Contacts button. In addition, both Mac and PC users should see a blue Upload Contacts button below a gray Choose File button.

   At this point, unless you've already done so, you need to create a contact file. If you don't know how to do that, click the How to Create a Contact File link above the gray Choose File button. A list of different e-mail programs appears with instructions for most desktop e-mail programs, as well as a few websites.
3. **Click Choose File.**

   A window appears allowing you to select the file from your computer's hard drive.
4. **Select a file and click Open.**

   The upload begins automatically. After your contacts are compared with Facebook's records, you'll be taken to Step 2 of the Friend Finder, Add Friends.
5. **Follow Steps 6 and 7 in the preceding section.**

Check out people you may know

After you have a friend or two, Facebook can start making pretty good guesses about others who may be your friends. Facebook primarily does this by looking at people with whom you have friends or networks in common. In the People You May Know box, you see a list of people Facebook thinks you may know and, therefore, may want as friends. People You May Know boxes appear all over the site. Usually the boxes include a list of names, profile pictures, and some sort of info like how many mutual friends you have or where the other person attended school.

When you find someone you know in the People You May Know list, click the Add Friend button or link by the person's name to add the person as a friend. If you're not sure, click the name or picture to see the person's Timeline and gather more information. If you're sure you don't know someone, or if you do know someone but are sure you don't want that person as your Facebook friend, mouse over the person's picture and click the X that appears. The person stops appearing in your People You May Know list. As you add or remove people from the list, more pop up to take their places.

Find classmates and co-workers

Friend Finder works by looking for large groups of people you might want to become friends with. A common assumption is that you'll want to become friends with people you've gone to school with and worked with over the years. To find these people, follow these steps:

1. **Click the Friends icon in the big blue bar on top.**

   The Friend Requests menu appears.

2. **At the top of the menu, click the Find Friends link.**

   The Friend Finder page appears.

3. **Click Other Tools.**

   A menu of possibilities based on information you've filled out on your Timeline appears.

4. **Click any Find Coworkers From or Find Classmates From links.**

   All these links go to the same place, which is a page for browsing people on Facebook.

5. **Use the check boxes on the left side of the page (shown in Figure 4-7) to look for people from your various jobs or schools.**

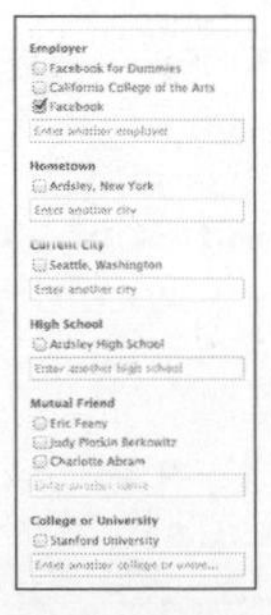

Figure 4-7: Use the check boxes to find your friends.

Selecting a check box displays people from that school or company. You can also look for people from your hometown, current city, or workplace by entering a mutual friend's name.

When you select more than one check box, you see *fewer* people because now Facebook is looking for people who both worked at Mom's Pizza *and* went to Hamilton High School. To find more people, select only one check box at a time.

You can browse for people in cities, companies, and colleges other than the ones you've listed on your Timeline. Look for the empty boxes that say Add Another, and type the school, city, or company where you think you know people.

Finding people with Search

Friend Finder is a great way to build your Friend List quickly. After you build it a bit, though, what if you find other people who may want to be your friends? Facebook Search offers you the capability to seek out certain friends by name.

The Search box in the blue bar lets you search a whole lot of things on Facebook: pages, groups, events, and even things your friends have liked. But most of the time, you use it to search for people.

Search can be a little confusing because Facebook autocompletes the names you type and assumes you're trying to get to your friends' Timelines. If you're used to pressing the Enter key to begin a search, you'll land on friends' Timelines when you meant to search for someone else.

You'll wind up using Search two basic ways. The first way is if the name of the person you're looking for (or someone with the same name) appears in the autocomplete menu. You can accomplish that sort of search following these steps:

1. **Begin typing the name you're looking for in the Search box.**

   Pay attention to the people who appear in the autocomplete menu. Facebook displays first your friends and then friends of friends.

2. **If you see the name in the autocomplete menu, use the mouse or arrow keys to highlight the name.**
3. **Click the name or press Enter.**

   You see the person's Timeline, where you can verify that you know the person and add him as a friend.

If you don't see the person you're looking for, don't despair; you can get more results:

1. **Type the person's full name in the search box.**
2. **Click See More at the bottom of the search menu.**

   The search menu expands to reveal new options.
3. **Click the People Named <*Friend's Name*> option.**

   A blue friend icon is next to this option. A search results page appears with larger previews of people's profile pictures and Timeline info. The right side of the page also has options for narrowing your search.
4. **Use the fields on the right side of the page to zero in on your friend.**
5. **When you find the person you're looking for, add her as a friend.**

Managing Friend Lists

After you do all the work of finding and adding friends, chances are you will see posts from people you find uninteresting. At this point, it's a good idea to get acquainted with the way Facebook automatically helps you end the madness, as well as some of the more specific and manual things you can do.

Friend Lists (capital *L*) are subsets of your giant list of friends (lowercase l). Confused yet? Friend Lists are a way of organizing your friends into lists to make your Facebook experience easier and more personalized. By organizing your friends into Friend Lists, you can

- **Share different types of information with different sets of friends.** For example, your best friends may get to see your party photos, and your family may get to see your wedding photos. This is a custom privacy setting you can use all over Facebook.

- **See a version of News Feed that shows only updates from people in that list.** Easily zero in on updates from a certain group of people, such as your family. You can choose to view only News Feeds from those people.
- **Use Friend Lists in Chat.** Display yourself as online or offline to different groups of people, or easily scan for certain types of friends currently online, such as carpool friends if you need a ride. For more, see Chapter 5.

Using Smart Lists

Smart Lists are the lists that Facebook makes on your behalf. These lists are created automatically based on your interactions with your friends and shared characteristics of your friends. Here are some common Smart Lists:

- **Close Friends:** Facebook creates this list based on things like people you interact with a lot on Facebook and people you appear in a lot of photos with.
- **Acquaintances:** The opposite of the Close Friends list. This list is meant to be a place where you can cordon off the people you don't know as well. One of the default privacy options when you post something from the Share box is Friends Except Acquaintances.
- **Restricted:** This list is for people you want to add as friends but don't want to see posts that are visible to friends. In other words, people on this list see only posts that you choose to make public.
- **Family:** Based on information you've entered about your family, they may show up on this Smart List.
- **<*Your High School*>:** If you've caught up with a lot of old friends on Facebook, a Smart List might be created so you can post photos from the reunion or share memories just with them.
- **<*Your college/university/workplace*>:** Similar to a high school list, depending on the information your friends have listed on their profiles, additional Smart Lists may be created for these groups.

Although Facebook is smart, it's not perfect, so you may have to edit these lists. The accuracy of the lists may also depend on how you want to use your lists. For example, you may want your Family list to make it easy to share with just your immediate family and, therefore, need to remove the more distant members. To edit a Smart List, follow these steps:

1. **From the Home page, look on the right side of the page for the News Feed menu.**
2. **Click the down arrow to expand the News Feed menu, and then click the See All link to expand the menu further.**

   All your lists appear, along with links to categories of News Feeds you can look at, such as Music.
3. **Click the list you want to edit.**

   You see that list's News Feed. On the right side of the page is an On This List section, where you can check out the current members of the list.
4. **To add people to a list, type their names in the text box in the On This List section.**

   Facebook autocompletes as you type. Select your friends' names when you see them.
5. **To remove people from a list:**
   a. **Click Edit in the upper-right corner of the On This List section.**

      A menu appears with options for changing what you see in this view.

   b. **Click Add/Remove.**

      A pop-up window displays the names and pictures of all members of the list.

   c. **Hover your cursor over the person you want to remove, and then click the X that appears. Repeat for each person you want to remove.**
6. **Click the Finish button when you're done.**

You can edit who is on a Smart List at any point in time.

Creating your own Friend Lists

Sometimes you want a specific list that Facebook can't figure out. This might be a sub-subgroup, like all the people you played Frisbee with in college. In these cases, create your own Friend List:

1. **From the Home page, click the down arrow to expand the News Feed menu (on the right) and then click the See All link to expand the menu further.**

   You see a list of all the ways you can view News Feed, including seeing only certain types of stories or only stories from certain lists.

2. **Click the Manage Lists option.**

   You see the Manage Lists page (a page that lists all your lists).

3. **Click the Create List button, in the upper-right corner.**

   The window in Figure 4-8 appears.

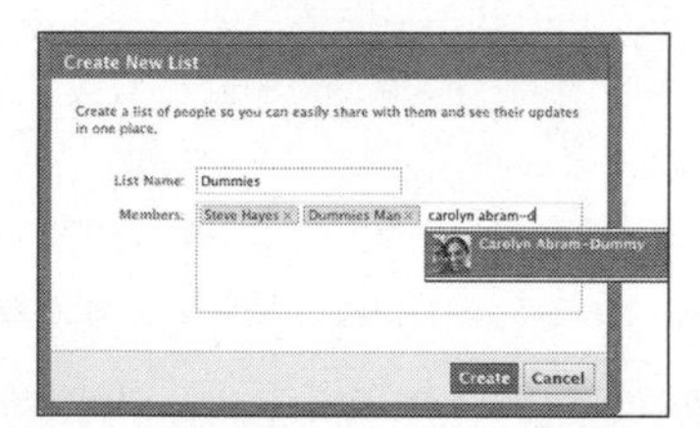

Figure 4-8: Creating a Friend List.

4. **In the List Name box, type the name of your list.**

5. **Add friends who belong on this list by typing their names in the Members box.**

   Facebook autocompletes as you type. Press Enter when you highlight the correct friend's name.

6. **Click Create.**

   Now, wherever Friend Lists appear on Facebook, you have access to the new list you created.

Friend Lists you create are private, so even if the list you're messaging is known in your mind as *Annoying Co-Workers,* all that your annoying co-workers see is a list of names. Members of Smart Lists are able to see the name of a list they've been added to.

Updating lists

After you create and start using your lists, you can add people to them when you add them as friends. When you're the one sending a Friend Request, follow these steps to also add the person to a particular Friend List:

1. **After you've added a friend, click the Friend Request Sent button on the friend's Timeline.**

   A menu appears asking if you want to add that person to any of your Friend Lists. Your most commonly used lists appear at the top.

2. **Click the list you want to add your friend to.**

   You may need to select Add to Another List to see your full menu of lists.

If you're the one receiving the Friend Request, you can follow these steps to add someone to a list as you accept the request:

1. **From the Friend Request menu, click Confirm.**

   This adds the person as a friend. The Confirm button changes to a Friends button.

2. **Click the Friends button.**

   A menu appears with some options about News Feed, in addition to lists you may want to add the friend to.

3. **Click the list you want to add this person to.**

   You may need to select Add to Another List to find the list you want.

If at any point you remember that you want to add someone to a list, simply visit that person's Timeline and click the Friends button, at the lower-right of the cover photo. The menu covered in the preceding steps appears, which you can use to add the person to the right list.

Selecting News Feed options

In addition to News Feed views, you can use News Feed options to control which friends' posts you see when you log in to Facebook. For example, if one of your friends changes her profile picture all the time, it might start to clutter up your News Feed. Similarly, I've heard lots of complaints about reading political screeds you disagree with during the election season. From your News Feed and from your friends' Timelines, you can control how much you see of your friend in your News Feed. You can also be specific, talking about the sort of posts you want to see from them (Yes to photos, No to status posts, for example). See Chapter 5 for details.

Following people

Occasionally, next to the Add Friend button on someone's Timeline, you'll see an additional button named Follow. Following people on Facebook is a way of getting updates from them in your News Feed without becoming their friend. To follow someone, navigate to that person's Timeline and click the Follow button. To unfollow the person, click that same button (it now says Following) and choose Unfollow.

Unfriending

Maybe you just feel like you have too many friends, or maybe you and a friend have legitimately drifted apart. Don't worry, because Facebook friendships are not set in stone. To unfriend someone, do the following:

1. **Go to the person's Timeline and click the Friends button.**

   A menu appears for assigning people to Friend Lists.

2. **Click the Unfriend link.**

   A window pops up asking if you're sure you want to remove this friend.

3. **Click the Remove from Friends button.**

   Take a moment of silence. Okay, that was long enough.

People aren't notified when you unfriend them, but people who care about you have a tendency to notice that, hey, you're not in their list of friends anymore. This can lead to awkwardness, so it might be worth using your privacy settings to further limit these people's knowledge of your life *before* you unfriend them.

Chapter 5

Keeping in Touch

In This Chapter

- Finding out what your friends are up to by reading News Feed
- Interacting with friends via comments, likes, and sharing
- Taking a trip down memory lane with Friendship Pages
- Sending messages to friends
- Chatting with friends instantly

The main way people keep in touch on Facebook is through News Feed, the constantly updating list of stories about content people are posting to their Timelines. I talk about News Feed at length in this chapter, and also about the ways you interact with what you see there.

You also discover Facebook Messages, which stitches together e-mail, texting, and instant messaging with a Facebook twist. I end the chapter with a discussion of Facebook Chat.

Your Daily News . . . Feed

News Feed is the centerpiece of your Home page. When you log in to Facebook, you see the familiar blue bar on top and the left sidebar, but mostly you see News Feed.

So what is News Feed? It's primarily a collection of stories by and about your friends. If that doesn't clarify things, here are some definitions for the definition.

- **Collection:** Depending on the number of friends you have and how often you (and they) use Facebook, you may see everything your friends have done or shared, or you may see only a fraction of your friends and only a fraction of the things they do and share. Luckily, you can change and influence what you see.

- **Stories by your friends:** Most of your News Feed will be posts people have made to their Timelines. These posts are things your friends actively want to share with you, so Facebook puts them on your Home page.
- **Stories about your friends:** Adding a friend, liking a Page, and sending an RSVP are the types of actions by your friends that appear as stories in News Feed.

News Feed is like a newspaper centered on you and your friends.

Your News Feed may also include public posts from people you follow or Pages you like.

Anatomy of a News Feed story

Figure 5-1 shows a sample News Feed story: a status update from a friend.

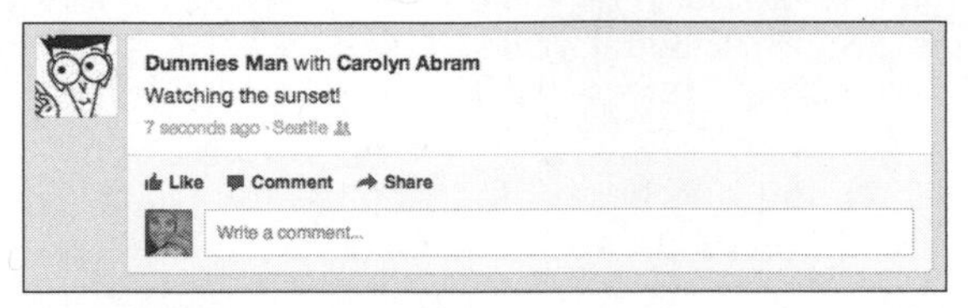

Figure 5-1: Just your average status update.

This tiny example contains six significant parts of the story:

- **Name and profile picture:** The first part of any story is who it's about or who wrote it. Both the name and picture are links to that person's Timeline. In addition, if you hover your cursor over a person's name, you'll see a miniaturized preview of the person's Timeline and buttons to message him and give him gifts.

Hovering your cursor over any bolded text in a News Feed story generates a preview for a Timeline, a Page, or an interest with specific buttons for adding friends, liking, or subscribing.

- **Content:** The content might be the status (as in Figure 5-1), a preview of an article, a video, or a photo album. It could also be a location where someone has *checked in,* or marked her location via GPS, using her phone. The content is the most important part of the story.
- **Tags:** Tags are a way of marking who is with you when you post something to Facebook. I'm using it here to include any of the additional info that may be appended to a post — location information or information about things you're doing, thinking, or feeling. Tags in posts are bolded. Hover your cursor over these tags to view more info about that person, Page, place, or thing.
- **Timestamp:** The little gray text at the bottom of the post tells you how long ago this post was added. In posts about photos, the timestamp often appears at the top of the post instead of the bottom.
- **Privacy Info:** The gray icon next to the timestamp represents whether your friend has shared this post with everyone (Public), just friends (Friends), or some other group of people (Custom). Hover your cursor over the icon to see who else can see the post.
- **Like, Comment, and Share:** These links allow you to interact with your friends about the content they've posted. In addition, you can see how many people have already liked a post, and you can see any comments that have been made below the post itself. Click Share to repost the content to your Timeline so your friends can see it in their News Feeds. In Figure 5-1, no one has yet liked or commented on the post.

Common story types

News Feed is made up of all sorts of stories. Although the basic anatomy is the same, here are some of the common story types you might encounter:

- **Status updates:** The status update post appears in Figure 5-1. Status updates are the short little posts that your friends make about what's going on in their lives.
- **Links:** Figure 5-2 shows a post sharing a link. Click the links (or the article's title) to go to the articles.

Figure 5-2: Use your status to share links to articles.

- **Photos:** Figure 5-3 shows a post about photos. When people add photos or are tagged in photos, it creates this type of post, with information about who was tagged and a sample of the photos that were added. Click the photos to see bigger versions and browse the entire album.

Figure 5-3: A photo story.

- **Videos:** Figure 5-4 shows a video story. Clicking the Play button opens the video viewer overlay where the video will begin to play. Videos from other sites, such as YouTube, often play right in your News Feed.
- **Timeline Posts:** Figure 5-5 shows a Timeline post story between two friends. The first person wrote the message on the second person's Timeline.

Figure 5-4: A video story.

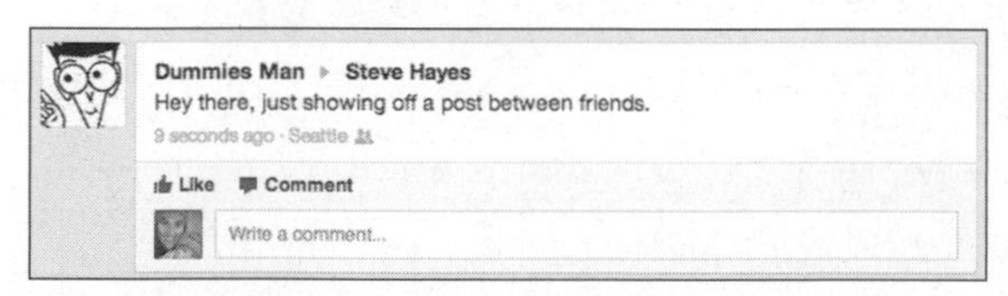

Figure 5-5: A Timeline post between friends.

You see Timeline post stories only when you're friends with both of the people involved. You won't see stories about a friend posting on a non-friend's Timeline.

- **Group and event posts:** When people post to a group or event you're a member of, the post may show up in your News Feed. These stories look similar to the Timeline posts, with the second friend's name replaced with the group or event name.
- **Check-ins/Check-in tags:** A check-in is something that you can do from your mobile phone or the Share box on News Feed or Timeline. It allows you (or your friends) to use GPS to mark, on Facebook, where you are. Check-ins are often accompanied by mobile photo uploads or status updates. For more about check-ins, see Chapter 7.

- **Likes:** Like stories are usually quick little stories that let you know what Pages your friends have liked recently. The Pages are linked so you can click right through to check them out yourself.
- **Read/Watch/Listen:** Certain services and websites, such as the book-reading site Goodreads, may be allowed to automatically post specific actions people take on their site to Facebook. See Chapter 8 for more information about how these applications work. Figure 5-6 shows an automated News Feed post from Goodreads.

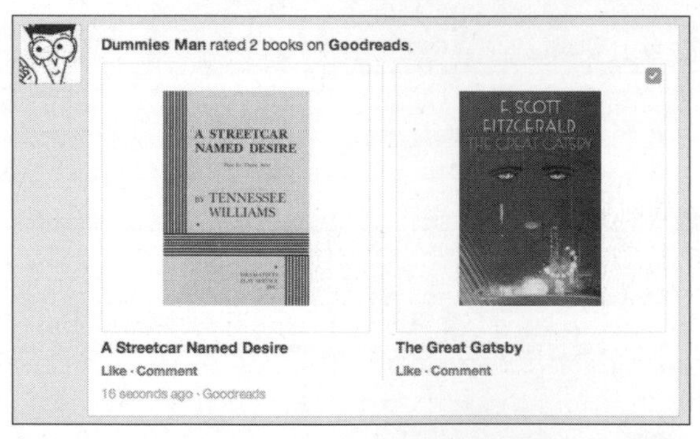

Figure 5-6: What are your favorite books?

- **Friendships:** Friendship stories might be about two people becoming friends or about one person becoming friends with lots of different people.
- **Changed cover and profile pictures:** These stories often look similar to a regular photo story. Click through to see the full-size photos on your friends' Timelines.
- **Events:** Stories about events (usually letting you know which friends have RSVPed *yes* to an event) include a link to the event. Only public events show up here, so if you've added a private event, don't worry about people who weren't invited seeing it in News Feed.
- **Most Shared:** If you follow certain Pages that post a lot of content and many of your friends share and reshare that content, you might find this sort of compiled story in your News Feed. A sample is shown in Figure 5-7. You can hover your cursor over any of their icons to see the most shared stories from their respective Pages.

Figure 5-7: Check out the most shared articles from your favorite publications.

- **Sponsored and suggested:** Suggested and sponsored stories are ads. Ads are what keep Facebook free to use, so there's no way to remove them.

Adjusting News Feed

News Feed is designed to learn about what you like and who you care about and to show you stories accordingly. Because there are limits to how well a machine can figure these things out, a number of tools can help you see more of what you like and less of what you don't.

News Feed views

Each *view* of News Feed allows you to control who and what appears in that view. To expand the News Feed menu, as shown in Figure 5-8, click the down-pointing arrow at the bottom of the News Feed box.

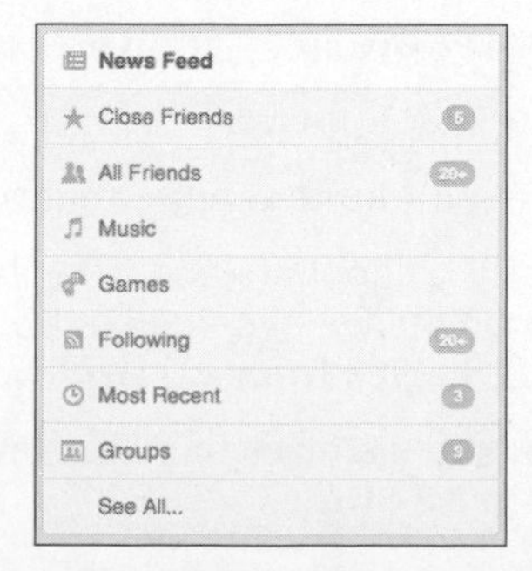

Figure 5-8: The News Feed menu lets you select different views.

The views of News Feed may appear in a different order depending on your own Facebook habits. You may also have to click the See All option at the bottom of the menu to view all your options:

- **All Friends:** News Feed pays attention to the stories you seem to care about most and over time culls stories from people you aren't as close to. If you do want to look at what *everyone* is up to, you can view All Friends.
- **Close Friends:** The Close Friends view shows you just stories from your closest friends.
- **Following:** This view of News Feed shows you posts from the people and Pages you follow.
- **Photos/Music/Games (not all pictured in Figure 5-8):** These options show you only photos, or only stories related to music your friends are listening to or like, or only stories related to games you and your friends may be playing.
- **Most Recent:** This view of News Feed is sorted solely by how recently something happened.
- **Lists:** Friend Lists appear in your News Feed menu so you can focus just on stories from any list you've created.

Hiding stories

While you can use News Feed views to look at a different version of News Feed, you can also influence what News Feed shows you by hiding stories you don't like. To hide a story, follow these steps:

1. **Hover your cursor over the story you want to hide.**
2. **Click the gray arrow that appears.**
3. **Choose Hide from the menu that appears.**

   The story immediately disappears and is replaced with two lines of text. You see two links in bold: **Unhide** and **Hide All Stories from <*Friend Name*>.**
4. **To never see the person's stories in your News Feed, click the link to Hide All Stories.**

If you want to unhide people from your News Feed, follow the preceding steps to hide all stories from a friend. A link appears to Edit News Feed Options. Click this link to display a list of all the people and Pages you've hidden. Click the X next to names you'd like to see in News Feed again, and then click Save.

Settings for friends

When you add a friend, you start seeing some of that friend's updates in your News Feed. To control the updates you see, you can adjust the person's News Feed settings:

1. **Go to the person's Timeline.**

   Use Search or click her name anywhere you see it around the site.

2. **Click the Friends button, and select Settings from the menu that appears.**

   The News Feed settings menu appears, asking which updates you want to see from that person.

3. **Decide how much you want to see from your friend:**

   - *All Updates:* Everything.
   - *Most Updates:* News Feed determines which stories from this person to show you.
   - *Only Important:* If you want to see drastically less of a person, this option usually does the trick, without the danger of missing big news.

4. **Decide whether you want to see a particular type of story.**

   The bottom part of the News Feed settings menu shows types of stories that appear in News Feed. Select any story type to remove its check mark.

Sharing Is Caring

You've probably noticed the word *share* used a lot on Facebook. In addition to the Share box at the top of your News Feed and Timeline, Facebook has a specific Share feature, designed to make it easy to post and send content that you find both on Facebook and on the web.

If you're looking at content on Facebook that you want to show someone, click the Share link near it. A pop-up window appears with a Share box (see Figure 5-9).

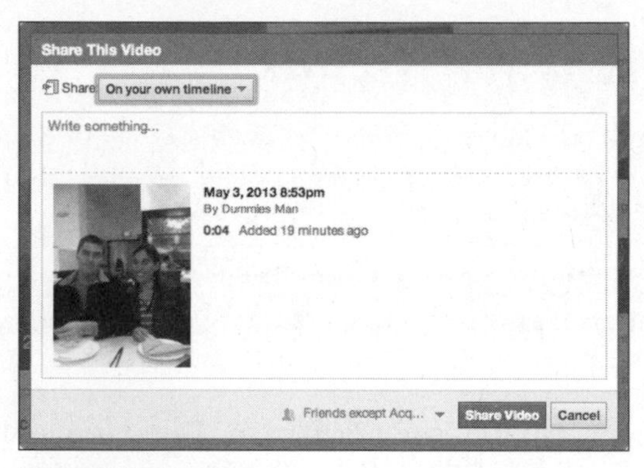

Figure 5-9: Share here.

The Share box has a drop-down menu for choosing where you want to share the content. You can share

- **On Your Own Timeline:** Post the content to your Timeline the same way you post a link or a photo from your Share box. The content will go to your friends' News Feeds as well.
- **On a Friend's Timeline:** Accomplish the same thing as copying and pasting a link into a post you leave on your friend's Timeline.
- **In a Group:** Post the content to a group you're a member of.
- **On a Page You Manage (for Page owners only):** Share things as a post from your Page if you're the admin of a Page.
- **In a Private Message:** Accomplish the same thing as copying and pasting a link into a message to a friend. Only the friend you send it to will see the link.

After you choose how you want to share the item, you can write something about what you're sharing. If you're sharing an article, you can edit the preview that appears in the post. Hover your cursor over the headline and teaser text to highlight them. Click the highlighted text to begin editing the preview.

Commenting and Liking

In addition to leaving a Timeline post, you can interact with your friends on Facebook by commenting on or liking the things they post.

Comments

To comment on anything on Facebook, first click Comment if the comment box is not expanded. Then click in the text box that appears, and type away. When you're finished, press Enter.

Frequently, comment *threads,* or a series of comments, can become like an ongoing conversation. If you're responding to someone who commented above you, type the @ symbol (Shift+2) and start typing the name of the person you want to respond to. You'll be able to select her name from an auto-complete list that appears.

After you comment on something, you'll be notified about subsequent comments so that you can keep up on the conversation. You can delete your comment by hovering your cursor over it and clicking the X that appears. You can do the same to a comment on something you've posted.

Liking

Liking is just a fast way for you to let your friends know that you're paying attention and like what you're seeing. To like something, simply click the word *Like* below or next to the item. Your friend will be notified that you like it. (If you didn't mean it, click Unlike.)

Liking Pages

You can like almost anything on Facebook. You can like a photo or a status; you can even like a comment on a photo or status. But there's a slight difference between liking this sort of content and liking Pages.

Pages are sort of official Profiles that companies, bands, and public figures make to represent themselves on Facebook. They mostly work like Timelines, except instead of friending or following Pages, you like Pages.

This sort of liking has a big implication: You may start seeing posts and updates from the Page in your News Feed, along-side stories from your friends. If they start to bother you, hide that Page from your News Feed.

Commenting, liking, and sharing across the Internet

If you're a reader of blogs, you may notice that the Comment and Like links and icons appear in lots of places. You can like posts on any website you're viewing, and those likes will be recorded on your Timeline and may appear in your friends' News Feeds.

Similarly, some blogs use Facebook comments as their primary commenting system. The way you comment is the same.

Sending a Message

Figure 5-10 shows the basic New Message window. I generated this one by clicking the Messages shortcut in the big blue bar on top (it looks like two overlapping word bubbles) and clicking the Send a New Message link from the menu. The New Message window then opened.

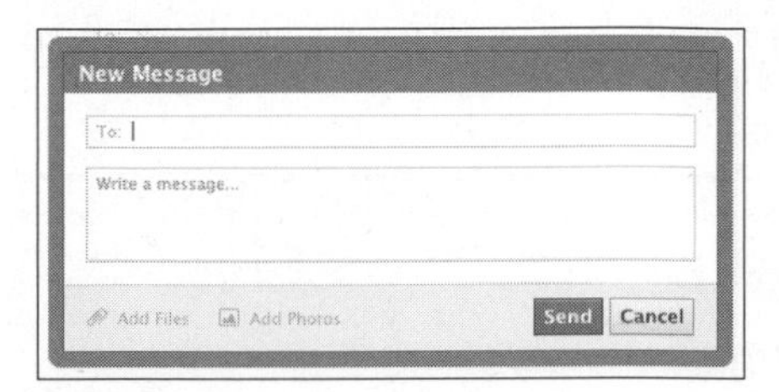

Figure 5-10: Send a new message.

To address your message, simply start typing the name of the friend you're messaging in the To field. Facebook autocompletes with the names of your friends as you type. When you see the name you want, highlight it and click or press Enter. To send a message to more than one person, separate each e-mail address with a comma.

You can send a message to people's e-mail addresses if they aren't yet on Facebook. Simply type the full e-mail address in the To field.

Type your message in the message box. If you want to add a link to a website or article to a message, you can copy and paste it into the message box. Facebook then generates a preview of the article so your friend has more info before clicking the link. When you're done writing your message, click Send.

You've Got Mail!

Chances are if you send out a message, pretty soon you'll get a reply. Depending on your settings and whether you're logged in to Facebook, when you receive a new message, you see either a new chat window open up (like you're receiving an IM) or a red flag on your Home page over the Messages icon in the big blue bar on top. Click the flag to open the Inbox preview; then click the message preview to be taken to a full conversation.

On Facebook, the series of messages between two people is a *conversation* or *thread.* This is because when you look at a message, it doesn't stand alone; rather, it is added to the bottom of all the messages, chats, and texts you have ever sent each other through Facebook.

In Figure 5-11, you can see a conversation between my friend Amy and me.

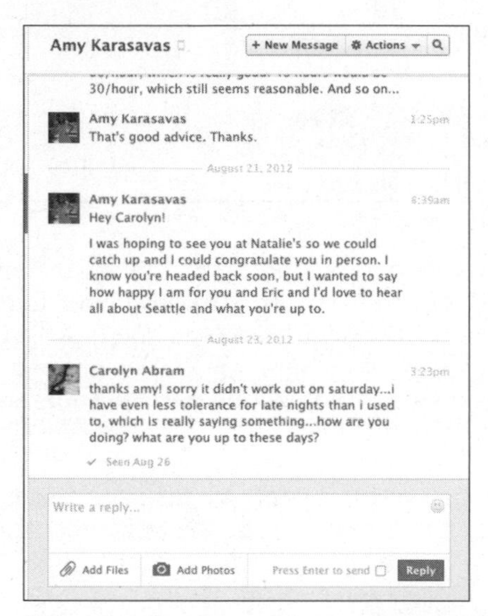

Figure 5-11: Carolyn and Amy converse on Facebook.

The most recent message is at the bottom. Unlike News Feed or Timeline, you scroll up to see older messages. In this case, if you keep scrolling up, you'll see an ongoing conversation that started three years ago, when Carolyn and Amy first became Facebook friends.

You may not always be messaging a friend from your computer. You may message a friend from your phone or chat via Facebook Chat (which I cover later in the "Chatting" section). No matter where the message is sent from, it's recorded in this ongoing conversation.

At the bottom of your conversation, below the most recent message, is the message composer. The To field is missing because whom the message is to is already clear.

Select the Press Enter to Send option (refer to Figure 5-11) if you want to send messages by pressing Enter. (If you need a paragraph break in what you're writing, press Shift+Enter.) Deselect the box to turn it off. When it is turned off, a Reply button appears. You click that button to send your message.

In the upper-right corner of the message reply box is a smiley face. Click it to open a menu of emoticon options (such as smiley faces and hearts).

At the top of your conversation page are the New Message button, the Actions button, and a Search button (the magnifying glass). Clicking the New Message button opens a blank conversation with a blank To field and an empty message box. Clicking the Search icon (the magnifying glass) opens a Search box you can use to search the entire conversation.

The Actions button features a drop-down list, as shown in Figure 5-12, with the following options:

Figure 5-12: Actions to choose for your conversation.

- **Mark as Unread:** Mark the conversation as having unread messages. The main Messages Inbox appears, and the conversation is highlighted in blue.
- **Open in Chat:** Open a message thread in Chat and send messages back and forth with your friend while you're browsing Facebook. A small chat window (covered later in this chapter) appears at the bottom of the screen.
- **Forward Messages:** Send some or all messages from this conversation to other people.
- **Delete Messages:** Like forwarding a message, this option allows you to delete some (or all) of the messages from any given conversation. After a message is deleted, you can never get it back.

Just because you've deleted a message doesn't mean your friend has deleted it. So if you send some private information and then delete the message, your friend can still see that information.

- **Delete Conversation:** Remove the entire history of messages from your Inbox.
- **Mute Conversation:** Mute a conversation (usually a group conversation) that is becoming more annoying than useful. For example, if you're in an ongoing conversation with some old friends to catch up, but the conversation turns to a local meet-up that you won't be able to make, you can mute the conversation. Check in every once in a while, and if the conversation grows more relevant, you can unmute it by clicking the Actions button and choosing Unmute from the options.
- **Move to Other:** If a conversation with someone doesn't deserve top billing among the messages you really care about, you can relocate it to the Other Inbox. When you're looking at a conversation in the Other Inbox, this option will be Move to Inbox.
- **Archive:** Choose Archive to send your conversation to the archives. This moves the conversation out of your main Messages Inbox until a new message is sent.
- **Report Spam or Abuse:** When you choose to report something, you can then
  - Mark the conversation as spam and move it to the Spam folder.
  - Report individual messages from a hacked friend as spam and delete them.
  - Report conversation participant(s) for harassing or threatening you.
- **Keyboard Shortcuts:** See a menu of keyboard shortcuts that do . . . nothing. As far as I can tell, it's a practical joke on the part of Facebook.
- **Feedback:** Go to the Help Center, where you can submit specific feedback to Facebook.

You can message more than one person at a time. Doing so creates a new conversation among all the people you message. Everyone can see and reply to the message. When you're looking at that conversation, you can see all the messages that have been sent by all the people involved. Figure 5-13 shows a conversation among several friends.

Figure 5-13: A group of friends conversing.

Much like the individual conversation, you can read this exchange from top to bottom, with the most recent message appearing at the bottom of the page. You can scroll up to read earlier messages.

Below the most recent message is a box for replying. The main thing to remember about group conversations is that you cannot reply individually to members of the conversation. When you reply, all members of the conversation see your reply.

The Actions drop-down list for group conversations offers a few more options not included for individual conversations:

- **Create Group:** If you find yourself talking with the same set of people all the time, create a group for a richer set of options for sharing. Groups make it easier to share and talk about things like links and documents.
- **Add People:** If you realize that someone else should be part of the conversation, choose this option to add him. You're asked to enter the name(s) or e-mail(s) of the person you want to add. The person added can see the entire conversation history.

- **Leave Conversation:** If a conversation isn't interesting to you anymore, choose this option to leave it. The other people on the thread will see a small notice that you have left.

Chatting

Sometimes you've got something to say to someone, and you've got to say it now. Try sending an instant message through Facebook Chat. Chat allows you to see which friends are online at the same time you are and then enables you to send quick messages back and forth with any one of those people, or have multiple simultaneous conversations with different friends. You'll find Chat in the bottom-right corner of any page on Facebook.

Whether a message or a chat, it all goes into your conversation history in your Messages Inbox.

Chat is meant to be quick and easy to use. When a friend sends you a chat, a small window pops up next to the Chat bar in the bottom right of your screen, as shown in Figure 5-14.

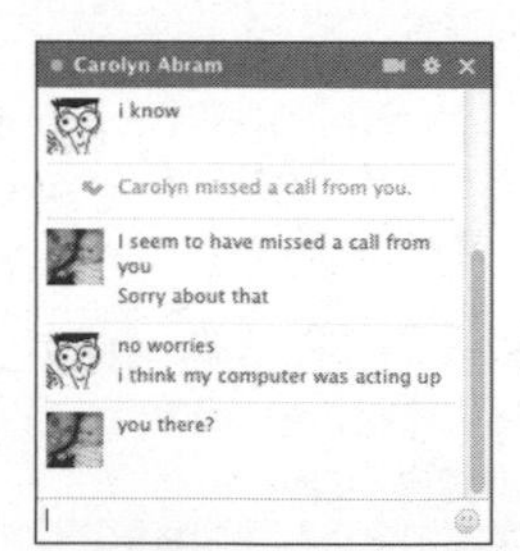

Figure 5-14: Someone chatted with you!

To send a chat message back, simply click in the text field at the bottom of the chat window, start typing, and press Enter when you're done. Your message appears below your friend's. Each new chat window lines up next to the other open ones. You can close an inactive window by clicking the X in the blue bar.

Because Chat and regular messages are integrated, when you begin a new chat with someone, your chat history is populated with your historical conversations, so your chat window tends to look a lot like a message thread.

To start a new chat with someone, you just need to select his name from the Chat menu. This opens a chat window that you can type in.

Chat options

At the top of each chat window is a blue bar displaying the name of the person you're chatting with and the gear and X icons. You may also see a video icon.

The X, farthest to the right, simply allows you to close the chat window at any time. Everything said is saved in your Inbox.

The gear icon, when clicked, opens a menu of options:

- **Add Files:** Search your computer for files you want to share.
- **Add Friends to Chat:** Add someone else to the chat. A new group chat window opens.
- **Turn Off Chat for <*Friend*>:** Friends may be more likely to chat with you when they see that you're online. If a friend is popping up a little too often, you can turn off chat for that individual person. From that point on, she will no longer see you in the Chat menu.
- **See Full Conversation:** Go to the Inbox view of your entire conversation history.
- **Mute Conversation:** If you find a chat thread growing annoying or irrelevant, mute the conversation to stop being notified whenever someone replies.
- **Clear Window:** If you find yourself wading through too much history at a time, select this option to get a blank slate of a chat window. Your full message history is still saved in your Inbox.

- **Report as Spam or Abuse:** If you're getting odd messages from a friend promoting something he wouldn't normally promote, there's a chance his account was *phished,* meaning someone who shouldn't have gained access to it. Report the spam messages to protect yourself, your friend, and other users from having the same thing happen to them.

Chatting with a bunch of people

To chat with more than one person, follow these steps:

1. **Begin a chat with a friend by selecting her name from the Chat menu.**

   This opens a chat window.

2. **Click the gear icon to open the Chat Options menu.**
3. **Select the Add Friends to Chat option.**

   A text box appears at the top of your chat window.

4. **In the text box, type the name of the friend you want to add.**

   Facebook autocompletes as you type. As soon as your friend's name appears, you can select it.

5. **Continue adding friends as needed.**
6. **Click Done.**

   This opens a new chat window for the group conversation. All messages sent in that Chat menu are sent to all participants.

This chat window has an additional icon, the Groups (overlapping people) icon. Click this icon at any point to add even more participants to your group chat.

Video Chat

Video Chat is a fairly new addition to Facebook, which is why you may or may not see the video camera icon at the top of each chat window. Facebook's Video Chat is actually powered by Skype, an Internet telephone service. If you see the video icon, you can initiate video chat with a friend. You can video chat with only one friend at a time:

1. **Begin a chat with a friend by selecting his name from the Chat menu.**

   This opens a chat window.

2. **Click the video icon to begin video chat.**
3. **If you haven't yet used video calling, click Set Up or Install from the window that appears.**

   This initiates a file download. Each web browser and operating system may have slightly different instructions. In general, you need to save the file to your hard drive and run it to complete the setup.

   After the setup is complete, a new pop-up window appears telling you that Facebook is calling your friend.

4. **Wait for your friend to pick up.**

   When he does, a video of him appears in a new window above Facebook. A video of you (what your friend is seeing) appears in the upper corner of this window.

5. **To end the call, close the window.**

Video Chat assumes both people have webcams either built in or installed in their computers.

Chapter 6

Presenting Photos and Videos

In This Chapter

- Looking at friends' photos and videos
- Adding your own photos and videos to Facebook
- Adding photos and videos from your iPhone or other smartphone
- Understanding privacy for photos and videos

Many Facebook users share the sensation of getting "lost" in Facebook — not in a bad way, but like you might lose yourself in a good book. It starts simply enough. You're looking at News Feed; then you click an appealing photo, which leads you to an album you like, which leads you to a video from a friend's vacation, which leads you to another friend who has a ton of new updates about her life. And the next thing you know, your editor is tapping you on the shoulder and saying, "Did you finish writing that chapter about photos yet?"

Facebook Photos is the leading photo-sharing application on the web. This may sound surprising because entire sites are dedicated to storing, displaying, and sharing photos, whereas Photos is just one piece of the Facebook puzzle. But the fact that *all* your friends are likely on Facebook and using Photos makes it a one-stop shop for tracking all the photos of you, all the photos you've taken, and all the photos of your friends.

Additionally, Facebook Photos allows you to add and share videos. Like photos, if you let videos languish on your hard drive or mobile phone, nobody gets to enjoy them. When you share photos and videos, they can become more cherished and more valuable as keepsakes.

Viewing Photos from Friends

Just by opening up Facebook and looking at News Feed, you'll find yourself looking at lots of people's photos. You'll see photos a few different ways: in your News Feed, in the photo viewer, and in an album format.

Photos in News Feed

Figure 6-1 shows an example of how a single photo appears in News Feed. Most of the screen is taken up by the photo. Running across the top is the name of the person who posted it and any description she wrote about it. There is also info about when the photo was added and how it was added (via mobile phone, for example). Below the photo are links to Like, Comment, and Share the photo. Beneath those links is the count of how many likes the photo has received and any comments people have made. You may even see a blank comment box, waiting for you to add your two cents.

Figure 6-1: Looking at a friend's photo in News Feed.

Clicking the photo expands the photo viewer, which is covered in the following section.

Figure 6-2 shows an example of a photo album preview in News Feed. It's similar to the single photo, but previews more of the photos from the album. The name of the album appears at the top of the post and tells you how many photos are in the album. Clicking any of the photos expands the photo viewer, and clicking the album title brings you to an album view.

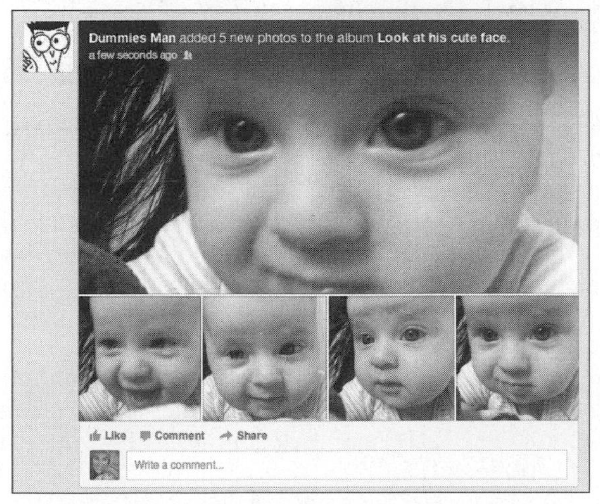

Figure 6-2: Looking at a friend's album in News Feed.

Photo viewer

The photo viewer allows you to quickly browse photos (and videos, but I get to that topic in the "Working with Video" section) and leave comments. Clicking a small version of a photo almost anywhere in Facebook expands the photo viewer and fades the rest of the screen to black, as shown in Figure 6-3. The photo appears on the left side of the viewer, and comments, likes, and info about the photo appear on the right.

Figure 6-3: The Photo Viewer.

When you hover your mouse over the photo, more options appear in white on the photo. On either side, an arrow allows you to navigate through a photo album. Clicking anywhere on the photo will also advance the album. At the bottom of the viewer, the following information appears:

- ***<Album Name>*:** The album's name is usually one your friend has created, like "Summer in February!," or a descriptive name generated by Facebook, such as "Mobile uploads."
- **Photo count:** The number of the photo in the album (for example, 5 of 8) is displayed.
- **Tag Photo:** You can add *tags* or labels for those in the photo. I cover tags in upcoming section, "Editing and Tagging Photos."
- **Options:** Clicking this option reveals a menu of options for things like downloading the photo to your computer, reporting the photo, removing a tag, or making a photo your own profile picture.
- **Share:** Post the photo to your own Timeline.
- **Like:** This option, like the Like link that appears on the right side of the viewer, lets the person who added the photo know that you like the photo.

The album view

The album view is the grid of thumbnail photos that you see when you click the name of an album or click a View Album link. Most average screens can fit about 8 to 12 photos in this view, and as you scroll down the page, more and more photos appear until you reach the end of the album. Sometimes if people add a large album, you may want to just skim an album view to see where the parts of the album are that interest you. Clicking on any one photo brings up the photo viewer.

At the top of the album view is the name of the album, some info about when and where the album was added, and any general info your friend has added about the album. Beneath the last row of photos, you can see who has liked the album or commented on it. Figure 6-4 shows an example album view.

Figure 6-4: An album view of photos.

Commenting on an album is different than commenting on a single photo. Leave a comment on an album to comment on the collection: "Looks like a great trip!" "Can't wait till we see the place ourselves." Comment on a single photo when you have something to say about that photo in particular: "Did you use a fisheye lens to get this shot?"

Viewing photos on your mobile device

Chances are that if you have a smartphone or a tablet computer like an iPad, you'll wind up looking at photos using the Facebook app. Looking at photos on these devices isn't too different from looking at them on a computer screen. Tapping a photo in News Feed expands the photo and fades the rest of the screen to black. Tap the photo once to see the options to like (thumbs-up icon), comment (comment bubble), or return to News Feed (Done button). Tapping the count of likes or comments expands a screen where you can scroll through the comments people have made on the photo. You can page through photos in an album just like you page through photos you've taken on your phone, swiping a finger from the right to the left side of the screen. The two-finger method of zooming in and out also works on Facebook photos.

Viewing tagged photos and videos of yourself

When I say *photos and videos of yourself,* I'm referring to photos and videos in which you're *tagged.* Tags are ways of marking who is in a photo — the online equivalent of writing the names of everyone appearing on the back of a photo print. Tags are part of what make Facebook Photos so useful. Even if you don't add lots of photos, other people can add photos of you. Photos you've been tagged in might be scattered across your friends' Timelines, so Facebook collects all these photos in the Photos section of your Timeline. You get there by clicking the Photos tab below your cover photo.

The Photos section defaults to showing Photos of <*Your Name*>. You can also view photos or albums you've added. The Photos of <*Your Name*> section shows the most recently tagged photos at the top of the page. As you scroll down, you see older photos of yourself. This is a great place to take a trip down memory lane and also to make sure that you're aware of all the photos of you that are out there.

If you've been tagged in a photo and you don't like that tag, you can always remove the tag. Then that photo will no longer be linked to your Timeline, and it won't appear in the Photos of You section of your Timeline either.

After you remove the tag, if you don't want a photo or video on Facebook, ask your friend to remove it. If you think it is offensive or abusive, you can also report the photo and ask Facebook to remove it.

Adding Photos to Facebook

Facebook is a great place to keep your photos and videos because it's the place where most of your friends will be able to see them. Whether that's a single photo you snapped on your phone or a big album detailing the latest family vacation, photos are most fun when you can share them and talk about them with your friends.

From the Share box at the top of News Feed, click the Add Photos/Video link to post photos. (You can also click the Photos link in the Share box at the top of your Timeline.) When you do so, you see something like Figure 6-5.

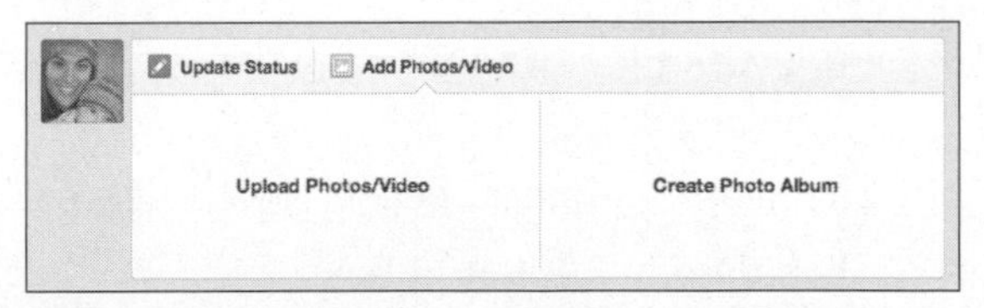

Figure 6-5: Choose how you want to upload your photos.

This screen gives you the following options for how you want to upload your content:

- **Upload Photos/Video:** Use this option if you have one photo you want to share or a few photos that you want to share and don't want to organize into a true album. You use this option also for adding videos, covered later in this chapter.
- **Create Photo Album:** Use this option when you want to show off a series of photos. Usually Albums are created to detail a particular event or period of time.

What's a tag?

Tagging — the part of Facebook Photos that makes the application so useful for everyone — is how you mark who is pictured in your photos. Imagine that you took all your photos, printed them, put them in albums, and then created a giant spreadsheet cross-listing the photos and the people in the photos. Then you merged your spreadsheet with all your friends' spreadsheets. This is what tagging does.

When you tag a friend, it creates a link from her Timeline to that photo and notifies her that you've tagged her. Your friends always have the option to remove a photo tag that they don't want linked to their accounts.

Tagging is most commonly used in Photos, but you can also tag friends in videos, status updates, and even in comments. All these little tags allow your friends to know when you're talking about them (good things, of course) or want to talk with them about something.

Uploading a photo

If you have a few photos you want to quickly share, follow these steps to get them out to your friends:

1. **Click Add Photos/Video in the Share box on your Home page.**

   The photo options appear (refer to Figure 6-5).

2. **Click Upload Photos/Video.**

   A window appears allowing you to browse your computer's hard drive and select the photo you want.

3. **Click the photo you want to share to select it.**

   You can select more than one photo if you want.

4. **Click Open or Choose (the wording may depend on your browser and operating system).**

   This brings you back to Facebook. A thumbnail of that photo appears inside the Share box.

Sometimes Facebook may be a little slow to add your photo. Blue progress bars may appear instead of thumbnails. You won't be able to post your photo until the photo has been added.

5. **Click in the Share box (where you see Say Something about This Photo) and type any explanation you think is necessary.**
6. **(Optional) Add tags, location info, and change the privacy of those photos from the options at the bottom of the Share box.**

   If you've never changed your Privacy settings, by default, everyone on Facebook can see this photo if they navigate to your Timeline. I usually like sharing my photos with Friends Except Acquaintances (see Figure 6-6). You can always choose a custom group of people who can and cannot see the photo.

Figure 6-6: Fill out info while your photos upload.

7. **Click Post Photos.**

   People will be able to see the photos on your Timeline and in their News Feeds (provided they're allowed by your Privacy settings to see the photos). By default, the photos are added to an album called Timeline Photos, which is basically a collection of all the photos you've ever added individually.

You can also drag and drop photo files from your desktop straight to the Share box, just like moving files around on your computer. After you've dragged a photo to the Share box, you can add a comment, a location, and tags, and change the privacy setting.

Creating an album

Whereas a single photo can share a moment, an album can truly tell a story and spark conversations with your friends. To create an album, follow these steps:

1. **Click Add Photos/Video in the Share box on your Home page.**

   The photo options appear (refer to Figure 6-5).

2. **Click Create Photo Album.**

   You see the same interface for exploring your hard drive that you used to upload a single photo.

3. **Select multiple photos by pressing the Ctrl or Command button and clicking the files you want.**

   If you use a program like iPhoto to organize your photos, create an album there first; then navigate to it and select all those photos to add to Facebook. That process is a lot easier than trying to figure out whether you want to use IMG0234 or IMG0235.

4. **When you're done, click Open.**

   The Upload Photos window appears (refer to Figure 6-6). The progress bar fills with blue as your photos are uploaded.

5. **Fill out Album Info.**

   As your photos upload, you'll see three empty text fields at the top of the page. Click Untitled Album to add an album title, click Where Were These Taken to add a location, and click Say Something About This Album to add a description of the album. You can click the Add Date link to add the date the photos were taken, which is especially useful if you're adding photos from the past and you want them to show up way back on your Timeline.

6. **Decide whether you want your photos shown in standard or High Quality resolution via the check box at the bottom of the screen.**

   High-resolution photos obviously look a bit better but take longer to upload. Unless you're a pro photographer or using a truly professional-level camera, standard quality is usually sufficient.

7. **Use the Privacy menu to choose who can see the album.**

   The Privacy menu reflects the privacy setting from the last time you posted something. For example, if you last posted something publicly, the Privacy menu displays the globe icon and displays Public.

8. **(Optional) After your photos finish uploading, add descriptions to individual photos.**

   The thumbnail of each photo has a blank space below it. Click into that space to add a caption or description of that individual photo.

9. **(Optional) Click on friends' faces to tag them. Type the name of the friend in the box that appears.**

   The tagging box is shown in Figure 6-7. You don't have to tag friends in your album, but tagging is highly recommended. It allows your friends to learn about your photos more quickly.

Figure 6-7: Who dat?

10. **Click Post Photos.**

    If Facebook's facial recognition software detects many photos of the same face, you may see a screen that shows you all the photos of that person and asks Who Is in These Photos? This allows you to make sure your friend is tagged in many photos without having to enter his name a zillion times. You may add tags here or skip to go to the album view of your album. After you get to the album view, you may rest assured that your album has been added to your Timeline and may appear in your friends' News Feeds.

Whew! That was a bit of a marathon. If you need a break or a drink of water, feel free to indulge. Then, when you're ready, jump to the "Editing and Tagging Photos" section to find out how to edit your album and the photos in it.

Adding photos from your iPhone

Lots of photos you see on Facebook are added when people are nowhere near a computer. Instead, they're the photos of things that happen while you're out and about. Things that are beautiful (spring blossoms!), or weird (how did this person lose only one high heel?), or just emblematic of your day (another cute photo of the baby).

If you add the Facebook app to your phone, iPhones and Android phones try to make it as easy as possible to send photos from your phone right to Facebook.

Here's a simple way to share photos if you're using an iPhone:

1. **From your photo gallery, tap the photo you want to share; then tap the Send icon at the bottom left of the photo.**

   A menu of options appears, including things like e-mail or text messages. If you previously installed the Facebook app, you should see the Facebook icon among the other options.

2. **Tap the Facebook icon.**

   A Facebook window for sharing that photo appears, as shown in Figure 6-8.

3. **(Optional) Use the keyboard to type any explanation the photo needs.**

4. **(Optional) Tap Add Location to use GPS to share where you're adding the photo from.**

Figure 6-8: Don't let your photos go unshared!

5. **(Optional) Tap the Privacy menu to change who can see this post.**

   Remember, by default, the audience you shared your last post with will be the people who can see this post.

6. **Tap Post in the upper-right corner of the Facebook window.**

   The photo is added to your Timeline as part of the Mobile Uploads album, and it may appear in your friends' News Feeds.

If you use an iPhone, you can download the Facebook Camera app specifically for taking and sharing photos. This app gives you tools like filters for your photos and makes it easy to look only at friends' photos.

Editing and Tagging Photos

After uploading a photo, you can still make changes to the way it appears on Facebook. If you added an entire album, you may want to add more photos or rearrange the order of the pictures. For any photo you added from a phone or just quickly from your computer, you may want to add tags, the date, or location information. Doing all this is relatively easy using the following common editing tasks.

Editing albums

Editing an album usually consists of editing the album's information or settings. You may also want to edit specific photos in an album. For those types of edits, hop on down to the "Editing a Photo" section.

Edit the album's name, location, description, and privacy

From the album view, look above the top row of photos for an Edit icon, next to the Add Photos button.

This little pencil icon always indicates that you can edit something.

Click the Edit icon to bring up the Edit Album screen (see Figure 6-9). It should look familiar — it's pretty much the same screen you saw when you created the album.

Figure 6-9: Edit your album's info.

The fields at the top are the same as when you created the album: album name, description (Say Something . . .), location (Where Were These Taken), and a Privacy menu. Remember to click Done when you finish editing this information.

From the album view, you can also click the pencil icon next to the existing description to edit it.

Delete an album

While you're looking at the Edit Album screen, look for a trash can icon. If you ever decide, in retrospect, that adding a particular album was a poor choice, you can click this button to remove the whole thing.

If you delete your photo album, all the photos in it will be gone forever, so make sure you want to get rid of it completely before you delete it.

Reorder photos in the album

Chances are that if you added your photos in bulk, they don't appear exactly in the right order. And it's awkward when the photos of the sunset appear first, and the photos of your awesome day of adventure come afterward. To reorder photos from the album view, follow these steps:

1. **Hover your cursor over the photo you want to move.**
2. **Click and hold down on the photo.**
3. **While holding the mouse button down, drag the photo thumbnail to its correct place in the album.**

   The other photos shift positions as you move your chosen photo (as shown in Figure 6-10).

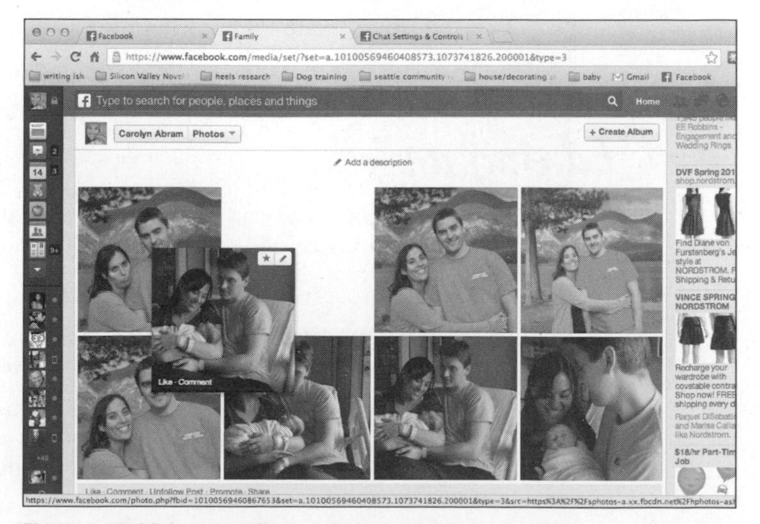

Figure 6-10: Make your album tell a story in the right order.

4. **When the photo is in the spot you want, release the mouse button.**
5. **Repeat with the next photo until your entire album is organized correctly.**

No need to worry about saving. Facebook automatically saves the new order of your album.

Add more photos to the album

After you create a photo album, you can add more photos later. Sometimes, depending on how organized the photos on your hard drive are, you may want to add photos in batches anyhow. To add more photos, follow these steps:

1. **Click the Add Photos button in the upper-right corner of the album view.**

   You see the interface for exploring your computer's hard drive.

2. **Select the photos you want to add.**
3. **Click Open.**

   The upload process begins, complete with a progress bar so you know how long the upload will take.

4. **Click the Done button after the upload is complete.**

   You're asked to tag the new photos you added.

Editing a photo

In addition to the actions you can take on an entire album, you can also take actions on individual photos within an album.

For all these possible photo edits, I assume you're already looking at the photo you want to edit in the photo viewer.

Add a tag to an individual photo

If you skipped adding tags earlier, you can always add your tags to individual photos.

1. **Hover your cursor over a friend's face.**

   The tagging box appears, as shown in Figure 6-11.

2. **In the text box, enter the name of the person you want to tag.**

   Facebook tries to autocomplete your friend's name as you type.

Figure 6-11: Tagging a friend in a photo.

3. **Repeat Steps 1 and 2 until everyone in the photo is tagged.**

   Or stop after you tag a few people. You can always come back to this later.

Rotate a photo

Lots of times, photos wind up being sideways. It's a result of turning your camera to take a vertical shot as opposed to a horizontal one. You don't have to settle for this:

1. **Click Options at the bottom of the photo viewer.**

   You see a menu of options related to that photo. Remember, you won't see this text until your mouse hovers over the photo.

2. **Click Rotate Left or Rotate Right from the menu.**

   You may have to click it more than once to get the photo properly oriented.

Add or change a description for a photo

Just like you can add a description to the album as a whole, you can add descriptions or captions to individual photos:

1. **Click the Edit button on the right side of the photo viewer.**

   A text box appears where you can edit the description.

2. **Enter your description in the text box.**
3. **(Optional) Add any tags.**
4. **(Optional) Add location information.**

   Facebook tries to autocomplete your location information as you type.

5. **When you're finished, click Done Editing.**

Delete a photo

Maybe you realized that all 20 group shots from the high school reunion don't have to go in the album, or that one photo has a whole bunch of crossed eyes. You can remove photos entirely from Facebook:

1. **Click the Options link at the bottom of the photo viewer.**

   A menu of options appears.

2. **Click Delete This Photo.**

   A pop-up window appears asking if you are sure.

3. **Click Confirm.**

   You're taken back to the album view, now with one less photo.

Automatic albums

Most of the time when you're creating a photo album, you decide what to title it and which photos go into it. There are a few exceptions to this rule. Facebook assembles certain types of photos into albums on your behalf. Most importantly, every time you change your profile picture or cover photo, Facebook adds it to the Profile Pictures or Cover Photos albums, respectively.

You can access this album by clicking your current profile picture or cover photo from your Timeline. You see the photo viewer, where you can click through your historical record of profile pictures. Even though Facebook created this album, you can still edit any part of it like any other album — you can caption, tag, reorder, and delete photos simply by clicking the photo you want to edit.

You can automatically turn any photo from this album back into your profile picture by clicking the Options link and selecting Make Profile Picture from the menu that appears.

Similarly, single photos that you add to your Timeline are collected in the Timeline Photos album. Photos that you add from your phone are added to a Mobile Uploads album. Videos also are collected into a Videos album.

Working with Video

Too often, videos wither away on hard drives or cameras or even on mobile phones. The files are big, and they can be difficult to share or e-mail. Facebook seeks to make sharing videos easier. So film away and then let everyone see what you've been up to.

Viewing videos

You'll mostly encounter videos in your News Feed with a big fat Play button in the center. Simply click that button to watch the video. It expands the photo viewer overlay, which makes the background darken and lets you focus on the video you want to watch. The video plays on the left side of the screen, and the right side displays the video's title, description, and tags, as well as links to like, comment on, and share the video. Any comments or likes that have already been made show up on the right side of the screen.

While the video is playing, you can hover your cursor over it to see the progress bar and to display the various links you can click related to the video. These elements appear in white toward the bottom of the video, as shown in Figure 6-12.

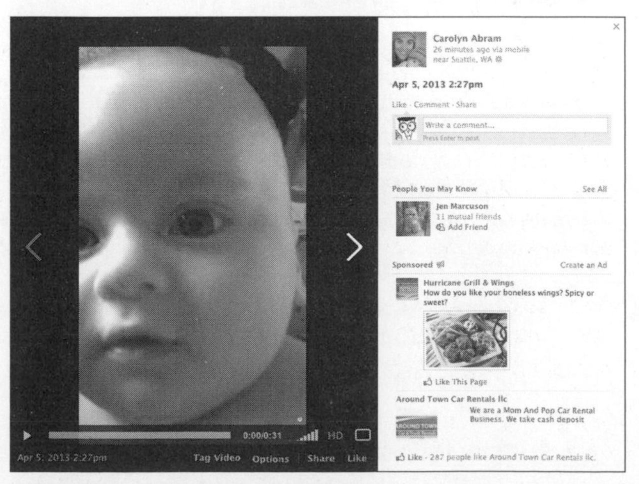

Figure 6-12: A video on Facebook.

Here are the components of the photo viewer when you are watching a video:

- **Progress bar, volume, and full screen:** Pause the video from the progress bar, as well as adjust the video's volume from the volume meter. Click the square icon to the right of the progress bar to expand the video and watch it on your entire computer screen.
- **Video title:** The video's title is at the bottom left of the viewer. If video doesn't have a title, the date and time of upload are displayed.
- **Tag Video:** Tag someone in the video.
- **Options:** View a menu of options, including a Report option if you ever see a video you think shouldn't be on Facebook.
- **Share:** Post a video to your own Timeline and share it with your friends.
- **Send:** Send the video to friends attached to a message. When you send a video, the message and video go to your friend's Inbox.
- **Like:** Let your friends know that you like their videos.

Adding a video from your computer

Uploading a video to Facebook includes going out into the world, recording something, and then moving it from your camera to your computer. I'm going to assume you've already done that part and are now back to being sedentary in front of your computer. Now, to upload a video to Facebook, follow these steps:

1. **Choose Add Photo/Video in the Share box at the top of your Home page or Timeline.**

   Options for adding photos and videos to Facebook appear.

2. **Click Upload Photos/Video.**

   A window expands so that you can navigate your computer's hard drive.

3. **Select a video file from your computer.**

   You return to Facebook, where your video is appended to your post. A filmstrip icon indicates that you're adding a video, not a photo.

4. **(Optional) Type an explanation or a comment in the Say Something about This Video box.**

5. **(Optional) Use the Privacy menu to select who can see this video.**

6. **Click Post.**

   A blue progress bar appears at the bottom of the post and you'll be notified that the video is processing. Uploading a video can sometimes take a while, so be patient. You can use Facebook in the meantime or edit the video's info. (Editing is covered in the "Editing and tagging videos" section, later in this chapter.)

Adding a video from your iPhone

Much like photos, many of the videos you want to share most are ones you take when you're out and about: someone attempting to park a car in a spot that's too small, your kid chasing a soccer ball, the bride and groom cutting the cake. More and more often, you may find yourself using your phone to record these videos.

You could move the video from your phone to your computer and then add it to Facebook, or you could skip the middleman and share it directly from your phone using the Facebook app:

1. **Tap the Photo option at the top of your mobile News Feed.**

   Your Photo and Video roll from your phone appears.

2. **Tap the video you want to add.**

   A preview of your video appears. You can play it here to make sure you want to share it.

3. **Tap the icon showing a blue pencil in a box, which appears at the bottom of the video preview.**

   The screen becomes the usual box you see when you add a status or other post, with a thumbnail icon representing the video. You can add a comment, a location, and tags, and change the privacy option just like you do for any other type of post.

4. **When you're done, tap Post in the upper-right corner of the screen.**

   The video is then added to Facebook. Your friends will be able to see it on your Timeline and in their News Feeds (depending on your privacy settings).

Editing and tagging videos

When I talk about editing videos that you've added, I don't mean the kind of fancy editing that editing software like Final Cut Pro might do. Rather, you're editing how these items are displayed and seen by your friends.

To get to the Edit Video screen, shown in Figure 6-13, click the Play button in the center of the video. This opens the Photo viewer overlay, where the video begins playing. On the right side of the viewer are three buttons: Tag Video, Add Location, and Edit. Clicking Edit turns the right side of the viewer into a series of text boxes where you can add information.

Figure 6-13: The Edit Video screen.

The Edit Video screen has several fields to fill out; most are optional:

- **Title:** Name your video. You can be artsy and name it something like *Boston Cream Meets a Bitter End* or something descriptive like *Pie in the Face*. If you don't choose a title, the video is automatically titled with the timestamp of when you recorded or uploaded it.

- **Description:** This field is for you to describe what's happening in your video, although frequently videos speak for themselves.
- **Tags *(Who were you with?)*:** This option is similar to tagging a photo or a post. Start typing the names of all the friends who are in the video and then select the correct friends from the list that is displayed. Your friends are notified that they've been tagged in a video and can remove the tag if they decide they don't want to be forever remembered as *The one who got pied in the face.*
- **Location *(Where was this video taken?)*:** You can enter a location such as a city or a place of business. Facebook attempts to autocomplete as you type.
- **Date:** As with any post, you can add a date to make sure it appears in the right place in your Timeline.
- **Privacy:** Your privacy options for videos are the same as for any post. By default, whatever the privacy was on your last post will be the privacy for the video you added. For all-around privacy info, be sure to read Chapter 3.

Click Done Editing when you finish filling out these fields.

Discovering Privacy

While privacy is covered in detail in Chapter 3, it's worth going over a few settings again now that you really understand what it is you're choosing to show or not show to people.

Album and video privacy

Each time you create an album, post a photo, or add a video to Facebook, you can use the Privacy menu to select who can see it. These options are as follows:

- **Public:** Anyone can see the album, but that doesn't necessarily mean that everyone *will* see the album. Facebook doesn't generally display your content to people who aren't your friends. But if, for example, someone you didn't know searched for you and went to your Timeline, she would be able to see that album.

- **Friends:** Only confirmed friends can see the photos or videos when you have this setting.
- **Friends Except Acquaintances:** People you've added to your Acquaintances list will not be able to see the photo or video. The rest of your friends will be able to see it.
- **Only Me:** Only you will be able to see that photo or video.
- **Custom:** Custom privacy settings can be as closed or as open as you want. You may decide that you want to share an album only with the people who were at a particular event, which you can do with a custom setting.

If you're new to Facebook and have never changed a single privacy setting, all posts you add — including photos and videos — are visible publicly by default. If you aren't comfortable with this, remember to adjust your Privacy settings accordingly when you add new photos and video.

Privacy settings for photos and videos of yourself

The beauty of creating albums on Facebook is that it builds a giant cross-listed spreadsheet of information about your photos — who is in which photos, where those photos were taken, and so on. You're cross-listed in photos that you own and in photos that you don't own. If you want more control over these tags and who can see them, go to the Privacy Settings page from the Privacy Shortcuts menu (which you access by clicking the lock icon next to your name in the left menu). From the Settings page, click the Timeline and Tagging section on the left side of the page.

The top two settings in the section labeled How Can I Manage Tags People Add and Tagging Suggestions are particularly relevant to setting privacy for photos of you:

- **Review tags people add to your own posts before the tags appear on Facebook?** Turning this option from Off to On means you get to make sure you want to be tagged in photos (and other posts) before anyone can see that you've been tagged. In other words, say that I tag my friend Eric in a photo.

  - If this option is Off, as soon as I tag him, the photo is added to his Timeline and (usually) his friends will be able to see that he's been tagged in their News Feeds.
  - If this setting is On, he has to approve the tag before it appears on his Timeline and in his friends' News Feeds.

- **When you're tagged in a post, who do you want to add to the audience if they aren't already in it?** Another way to limit who can see that you've been tagged in a post is to change this setting from Friends to Only Me or Custom.

  By default, if I tag Eric in a photo, his friend Dave, whom I'm not friends with, will be able to see the photo. If Eric changes this setting to Only Me, when I tag Eric, Dave still will not be able to see that photo.

Additionally, the Who Can See Posts You've Been Tagged in on Your Timeline setting allows people to tag you in photos, but prevents certain groups of people from seeing those photos on your Timeline. So, if I tag Eric in a photo that I shared publicly, someone he isn't friends with who visits his Timeline wouldn't see that photo unless Eric allows everyone to see posts he's been tagged in.

Chapter 7

Facebook on the Go

In This Chapter

- Capturing and sharing the moment with Facebook Mobile uploads
- Keeping yourself connected with Facebook Mobile Text
- Staying up-to-date with Facebook Mobile
- Discovering Facebook Mobile apps designed to work on your phone

Throughout this book, you discover how Facebook enriches relationships and facilitates human interaction. But what can Facebook do to enrich your relationships when you're *not* sitting in front of a computer? Life is full of beach weekends, road trips, city evenings, movie nights, dinner parties, and so on. During these times, as long as you have a mobile phone, Facebook still provides you a ton of value.

Don't take this as license to ignore a group of people you're actively spending time with to play with Facebook on your phone (unless, of course, you *want* to ignore them). Moreover, don't think you can tune out in class or in a meeting to poke your friends. But knowing the ins and outs of Facebook Mobile can enrich each experience you have — while you're having it. With Facebook Mobile, you can show off your kids' new photos to your friends or broadcast where you're having drinks, in case any of your friends are in the neighborhood and want to drop by.

Facebook Mobile serves another function — making your life easier. Sometimes you need *something,* say, a phone number, an address, or the start time of an event. Maybe you're heading out to have dinner with your friend and her boyfriend whose name you can't, for the life of you, remember. Perhaps you hit it off with someone new and would like to find out whether she's romantically available before committing yourself to an awkward conversation about exchanging phone numbers. In this chapter, I assume that you have a mobile phone and know how to use its features. If you don't have a phone, you may consider buying one after reading this chapter; this stuff is way cool. Mobile Texts simply require that you own a phone and an accompanying plan that enables you to send text messages. Facebook Mobile requires a mobile data plan (that is, access to the Internet on your phone). Facebook Mobile applications require that you own any one of the several types of phones or devices that Facebook can currently support.

Is That Facebook Mobile in Your Pocket?

In many ways, using a mobile phone can augment your experience of using Facebook on the computer. This first section is about how you can easily add information to and get information from Facebook when you're on the go and not physically in front of the computer. These features are primarily for people who do most of their Facebooking on the computer, but sometimes interact through their phone.

Getting started

This chapter gives you almost everything you need to know about using Facebook with a mobile device. However, if you ever find yourself asking questions about it while near a computer but *not* near this book, you can go to `www.facebook.com/mobile` for much of the same information. To get started with Facebook Mobile, you first need to enter and confirm your phone number in the Settings page:

1. **Choose Settings from the Account menu (down arrow) in the upper-right corner of the big blue bar on top.**
2. **Click the Mobile tab on the left side of the page.**
3. **Click the green Add a Phone button.**

   You may be prompted to reenter your Facebook password. When that's all squared away, the Activate Facebook Texts dialog box appears.

4. **Choose your country and your mobile carrier.**

   If your carrier isn't listed, you may be out of luck using Facebook from your mobile phone.

5. **Click Next.**

   This brings you to Step 6, which you have to do from your phone.

6. **From your phone, text the letter** F **to 32665 (FBOOK).**

   FBOOK texts you back a confirmation code to enter from your computer. This process can take a few minutes, so be patient.

7. **Enter your confirmation code in the empty text box.**

8. **Choose whether you want your phone number added to your Timeline via the Share My Phone Number with My Friends check box.**

   I find it useful when friends share their mobile numbers on Facebook because it allows me to use Facebook as a virtual phonebook. If you're not comfortable with that, simply deselect the check box.

9. **Click Next.**

   Your phone is confirmed.

Mobile Texts

After your phone is confirmed, Mobile Texts are the most basic way to use Facebook on your phone. You don't need a camera on your phone or a smartphone to use Mobile Texts. Using just a simple Short Message Service (SMS) or text message, you can update your status to let people know where you are and what you're up to.

Here are the various actions you can take on Facebook via SMS:

- **Update your status:** Type any sort of phrase in a text message. Your status will appear on your Timeline and in your friends' News Feeds with a little mobile icon next to it so people know you're on the go.
- **Add a new Facebook friend.** Send the word *add* followed by the person's name or the word *add* followed by the person's phone number. Using your phone to

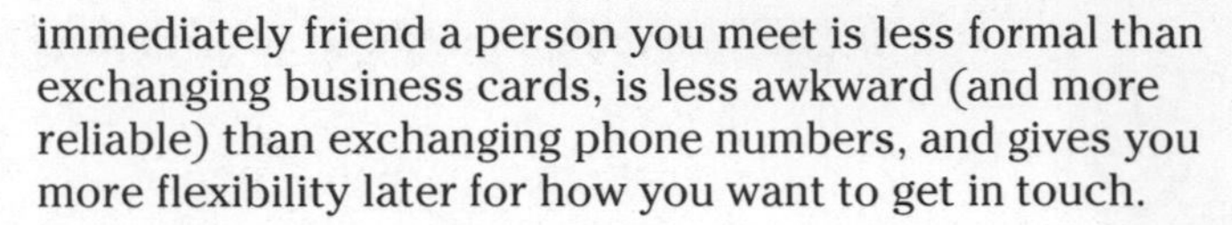

immediately friend a person you meet is less formal than exchanging business cards, is less awkward (and more reliable) than exchanging phone numbers, and gives you more flexibility later for how you want to get in touch.

Friending someone from your phone has all the same implications as friending someone from your computer, so friend wisely.

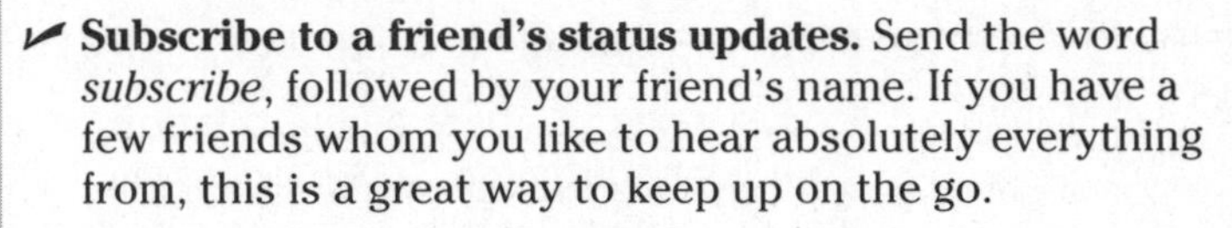

- **Subscribe to a friend's status updates.** Send the word *subscribe*, followed by your friend's name. If you have a few friends whom you like to hear absolutely everything from, this is a great way to keep up on the go.

If you subscribe to a lot of friends' statuses, make sure you have unlimited texting; otherwise, charges could pile up quickly.

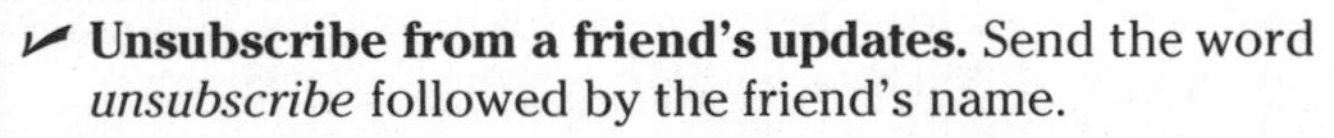

- **Unsubscribe from a friend's updates.** Send the word *unsubscribe* followed by the friend's name.

If you realize you want fewer people's statuses sent to your phone, just unsubscribe from the ones you don't want to see regularly.

- **Stop getting texts.** Text the word *stop*.
- **Restart getting texts.** Text the word *on*.

What's all the buzz about?

An old wives' tale claims that when you feel your ears burn, someone is thinking about you. Here's a slight modification: Someone, somewhere, is thinking about you when your phone starts vibrating. Turning on Facebook Mobile Texts means that you can be notified via SMS when someone requests to be your friend, sends you a Facebook message, comments on your photos, writes on your Timeline, or pokes you.

If you haven't already, you can activate Facebook Mobile Texts from the Mobile tab of the Settings page. To start, click the green Activate Text Messaging button. The next few steps should look familiar; they're the same as the ones you took to add your phone number. Figure 7-1 shows your Mobile tab after texts are turned on. You probably notice a few new settings that weren't there before. Click the Edit link next to each setting to change it.

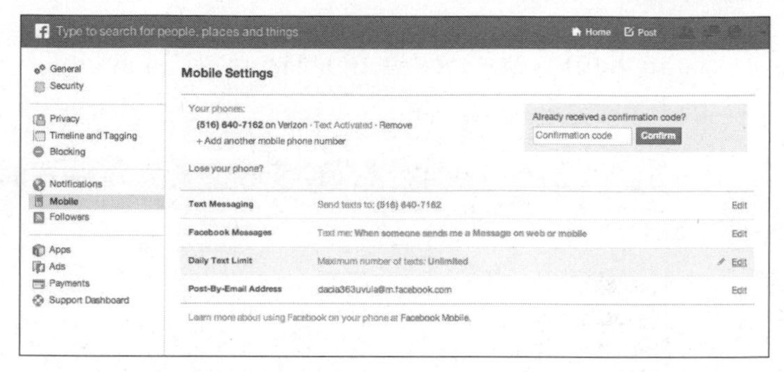

Figure 7-1: Set your preferences for receiving texts on your mobile phone.

- **Text Messaging:** Decide which phone number you want your texts to be sent to. You need to change this setting only if you have more than one mobile phone number listed for your account.
- **Facebook Messages:** Click Edit to open a drop-down menu where you can specify which actions warrant a text. You can choose to receive a text whenever someone sends you a Facebook message from either his computer or his mobile phone, whenever someone sends you a Facebook message just from his mobile phone, or never.
- **Daily Text Limit:** The Daily Text Limit allows you to modify the number of text messages you receive per day. Remember to click Save Changes after updating this setting.

If you have a mobile plan for which you're charged per text message (and you're exceedingly popular), use the settings that limit the number of messages Facebook sends you per day. Otherwise, you may have to shell out some big bucks in text message fees.

- **Post-By-Email Address:** Your Post-By-Email address enables you to upload photos and videos to Facebook from your phone. Check out the "Mobile uploads" section of this chapter for more information on how to post photos and videos via e-mail.

Mobile notifications

Just when you thought you were done with Mobile Text settings, I introduce a whole 'nother bunch of settings to further fine-tune your Mobile Texts experience. To get started, head to the Notifications tab of the Settings page and click Edit next to the Text Message section. Figure 7-2 shows this expanded menu.

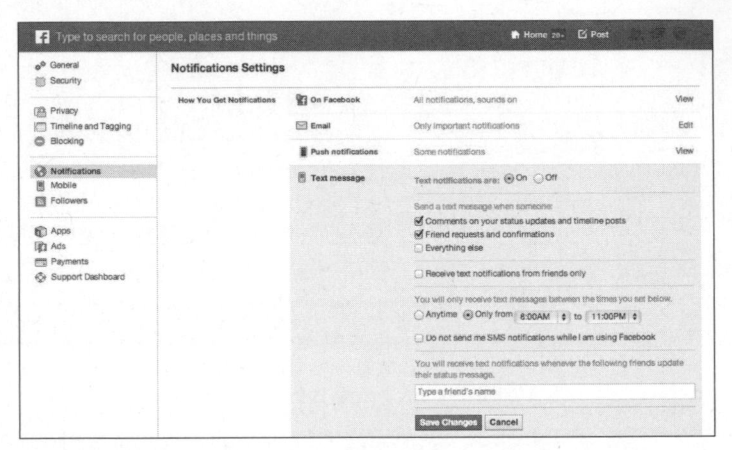

Figure 7-2: Tweak your Mobile Texts settings until they're just right.

From this section, you can change the following settings:

- **Turn text notifications on or off.** Fairly self-explanatory, although it's worth noting that even if you turn off Mobile Texts, you can continue to use the SMS commands I describe earlier in this section to update your status, add a new friend, and so on.
- **Decide which actions are text-worthy.** Choose to be notified when someone comments on your posts or status updates, when you receive a Friend Request or have a Friend Request you sent confirmed, and everything else, which encompasses actions like being tagged in a photo or receiving an Inbox message. You can select anywhere between none to all three of these options.
- **Receive text notifications from friends only.** This check box controls whether you want to receive a text only when you receive an Inbox message from a friend. For example, if a non-friend sends a message to your Inbox, you will not be notified by text.

- **Text times:** From here, you can specify a window of time when you'll gladly receive text notifications. So, for example, if someone pokes you at 2 a.m., you don't have to wake up for it. (Maybe you want to know *only* who's trying to poke you at 2 a.m. No judgment here.)

  Additionally, you can opt not to receive text notifications (via the Do Not Send SMS Notifications check box) while you're actively using Facebook because that can get a bit redundant.
- **Which friends' status updates should go to my phone?** This is another channel for specifying which of your friends' statuses you want sent to your phone. Simply type the name of the friend you want to subscribe to in this text box and choose the correct name from the auto-complete menu Facebook generates.

If you subscribe to the status of someone who doesn't spell very well but is conscientious about it, you may receive several texts as he tries to get his status just right.

Mobile uploads

Two types of people can be found at social events. The scrapbookers always remember to bring their fancy-schmancy camera to every gathering. (You know who they are because they tell you to smile a lot or sometimes say "Act natural.") The other people never intend to take photos but are ready with their mobile phone camera when the birthday girl blows out her candles, the host spills wine on himself, or someone arrives wearing a hilarious T-shirt.

To the scrapbookers of the world: Facebook Photos was built for you, so be sure to read Chapter 6 to get the most out of Facebook Photos. However, if you're the mobile photo taker, Mobile Photos is for you. With no time for weeding, editing, or second thoughts, mobile photos allow for instantaneous documentation.

Here's how to upload a mobile photo:

1. **Make sure you have a phone with a camera and you know how to use it to take a picture or a video.**

If you're unsure, check your phone's instruction manual or ask just about any teenager.

2. **Go to the Mobile tab of the Account menu and look for your personalized Post-By-Email address toward the bottom.**

   This e-mail address, such as `dacia363uvula@m.facebook.com`, makes it possible for you to upload photos to your Timeline from your phone. Be sure to add the e-mail address to your phone's contacts so you can easily message it in the future.

3. **Wait for something hilarious or beautiful to happen and then take a picture or video of it.**

4. **Send an e-mail to your address with the picture or video attached.**

   The subject line is the caption, so choose wisely.

5. **(Optional) Make changes to your mobile photo or video.**

   To do so, go to your photo albums and click the Mobile Uploads album or the Video album, respectively.

The default visibility of your mobile uploads is Public/Everyone.

Checking In

These days, most mobile devices have some sort of built-in GPS functionality, so you can use your phone to easily locate yourself on a map. Facebook Places is a way for you to connect to your friends who are physically nearby.

Facebook Places works like this: When you go someplace using your Facebook app or Facebook Mobile, you choose from a list of possible locations. These might be restaurants or parks or buildings. Facebook generates this list based on the location it's getting from your phone. When you select a location, you *check in* to that location. Checking in basically means actively telling Facebook that you're there. Facebook won't share your location unless you check in.

You can tag friends in your check-ins or add photos or a few words about what's going on. After you check in, your friends can see where you are in their News Feeds. If they're out and about and also using Facebook on their phones, they can see if they are near you by tapping Nearby from the Facebook menu.

Checking in to Places leads to all sorts of nice serendipitous encounters. When I was in Boston recently, I checked in to a few different restaurants. An old friend I hadn't seen in ten years sent me a message asking how much longer I'd be in town. I didn't even know she had moved to Boston. We had brunch the next day.

To check in from your iPhone, follow these steps:

1. **Tap Check In at the top of News Feed.**

   This brings up a list of nearby places. These places may range from official businesses (Peet's Coffee) to people's homes (Carolyn and Eric's Place) to shared spaces (Dolores Park, San Francisco Airport Terminal 2).

2. **Select the name of the place you want to check in to.**

   If you don't find what you're looking for, type the name of the place you want to check in to in the search bar above the list of suggested locations. If it's not found, Facebook brings you to the Add a Place page, shown in Figure 7-3, and you can tap the Add button to add the place to the list.

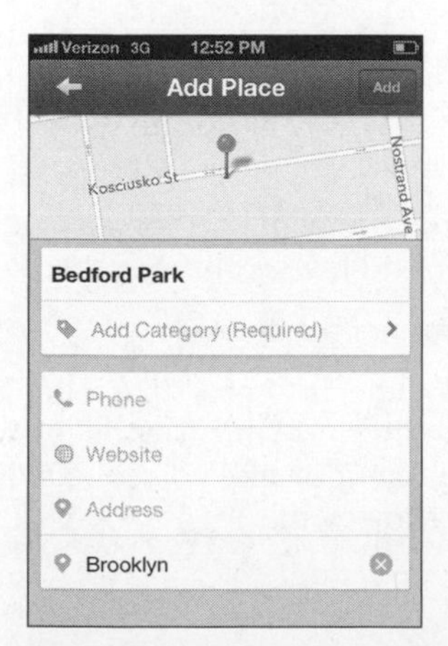

Figure 7-3: The Add Place page.

3. **(Optional) Type a comment in the Check In box.**

   The Check In screen appears, as shown in Figure 7-4. Check-ins with comments tend to feel a lot like status updates, with a little additional information.

Figure 7-4: Tell people where you are and why.

4. **(Optional) Tag friends by tapping the person icon and then tapping your friends in the list that appears.**

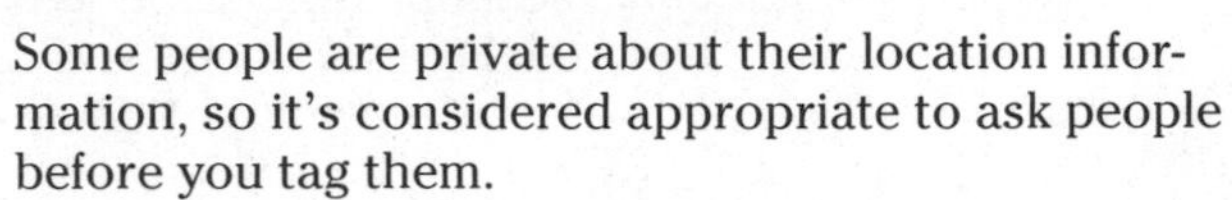

   Some people are private about their location information, so it's considered appropriate to ask people before you tag them.

5. **Tap Done when you're done tagging.**
6. **(Optional) Tap the Privacy menu to choose who can see this post.**

   You can choose from the usual options as well as choose from any Friend Lists you've created.

7. **Tap Post in the upper-right corner.**

   This officially marks you as "here." The check-in is added to your Timeline and your friends' News Feeds, where they can comment or like your check-in, or maybe even pop by to say hi.

Additional Mobile Apps

iPhone and Android users have a few other Facebook Mobile apps available to them. Each of these apps offers a pared down version of Facebook that focuses on one or two features or functionalities. Read on for a brief description of these apps.

Facebook Camera (iPhone only)

If you find photos to be the most engaging part of Facebook, you may want to download this application, which organizes all your friends' photo stories into a single photos feed. You can also post your own photos from the app.

Messenger (iPhone and Android only)

If you use Facebook Inbox as your personal messaging center, you may want to check out this app, which allows you to text friends using your phone's data plan as well as help you stay on top of multiple message threads via in-app notifications.

Facebook Poke (iPhone only)

With Facebook Poke, you can send pokes, messages, photos, and videos to individual friends or groups of friends. These features don't seem too exciting until you learn that if you send a message, photo, or video, you can choose the length of time (from one to ten seconds) that the content will be available for your friends to view. After the time has elapsed, the content disappears from the app.

A final word to the wise. If you use multiple versions of Facebook (computer, mobile, mobile app), you may find yourself inundated with repetitive notifications about the same action. For example, if my friend posts a photo to my Timeline, I might receive one notification in my e-mail, another through my phone's push notifications, and still another in the Facebook app. To cut down on the potential spam, go to the Notifications tab of the Account menu and adjust the settings in the How You Get Notifications section.

Chapter 8

Games, Apps, and Websites

In This Chapter

- Understanding what apps are and how they work on Facebook
- Seeing how apps can enhance your Internet experience on and off Facebook
- Discovering good, trustworthy apps

If you're familiar with Apple's iPhone commercials, you've probably heard the phrase, "There's an app for that." In iPhone-land, an *app* is a kind of program you add to your phone that suits your particular needs. It might help you track what you eat, or it might be a game you can play alone or with friends. iPhone apps take something that is already useful (your phone) and make it even more useful and fun.

Similarly, apps on Facebook take something that is already useful (Facebook) and make it even more useful and fun. They can take advantage (with your permission) of some of the parts of Facebook that are hard to replicate elsewhere, things like your Friend List, the things you like, and News Feed.

On Facebook, apps can exist for a whole host of reasons. They may be related to sharing things like what you're reading or listening to. They can be games you can play with your friends — both on Facebook and on your mobile phone. And they are found on other websites, because you can use your Facebook information, like your name and profile picture, to skip setting up multiple profiles on multiple sites.

Understanding What an App Is

For a long time, Facebook was the only company that could build apps for Facebook. And it did; it built Photos, Events, and Groups. All these are considered applications because they use the same core set of information to function: the connections between you and your friends. Building these apps on Facebook made them easier for people to use and also better. Using Facebook Photos is great because of tagging — the connections between the people in them. Events and Groups are great because the invite lists are easy to access, and you know who everyone is. Additionally, News Feed spreads information about photo tags and events and so on, meaning more people can find out about cool things.

The thing to remember about the apps and games I talk about in this chapter, however, is that they weren't built by Facebook. Why does this matter? It matters because sometimes some apps may behave differently than Facebook does. Things may look or function differently, and unfortunately, sometimes the apps you use may be less inclined to offer you a useful product and more inclined to spam you (and your friends) or do shady targeting with your information. That's why when you use applications, you need to authorize their use of your information. You should also know how to get rid of applications that are behaving badly (which I cover in the "Managing Your Apps" section).

Getting Started

Getting started using an app is often as simple as clicking a button. A lot of things happen behind the scenes when you click those buttons.

What apps need from you

Before you can start using most applications in Facebook, you need to grant the applications permission to interact with your Timeline, account, and information. When you start using a new app, you must grant it permission to access your information.

The basics

All apps need your basic information and your e-mail address if you want to use them. In other words, if you're not comfortable sharing this information with an app, you can't use it. Your *basic information* refers in this case to any information about you that is set to Public. For everyone on Facebook, this includes

- Your name
- Your profile picture
- Your gender
- Your user ID (This is the number associated with your Facebook account; everyone has a unique ID.)
- Your list of friends
- Any other information you have shared publicly

In addition to this, when you start using a game or app, most apps will request that you share your contact e-mail address with them. The app will be allowed to store that e-mail address to contact you in thc future. In this way, the developers can always get in touch with you, without Facebook acting as an intermediary.

Giving your e-mail to an application means you can get e-mail newsletters and other updates direct from the source without logging in to Facebook. If at any time you don't want to share your e-mail address with a certain application anymore, you need to unsubscribe from its e-mail list through *the app developer* as opposed to through Facebook.

The slightly less basic

In addition to basic information, apps might require specific types of information that is not publicly available. What information this includes depends entirely on the app and what it does. Here are some examples of information an app might want to use:

- Things you like (books, music, movies, Pages, and so on)
- Things your friends like (books, music, movies, Pages, and so on)
- Your location

- Your birthday
- Your photos
- Your posts
- Posts that have been shared with you
- Other profile info, such as your education, work history, and relationship information

Permission to act

In addition to all the types of information apps need from you, apps also need permission to take certain actions, including things such as the following:

- Posting to your Timeline on your behalf (for example, creating a post when you win a game). You can choose who can see these posts using the regular Privacy menu, which I discuss at length in Chapter 3.
- Accessing your information when you're offline (for example, looking up some of the information just listed, even when you aren't using the app).

App Install Screen

The *App Install Screen* is a blanket term I use to refer to the place where you're notified that an action (such as clicking a button) will share your information with an app. For example, if you click a News Feed story, an alert window might pop up asking whether you want to continue playing a game. Figure 8-1 shows one incarnation of the App Install Screen; in this case, it's on the right side of an app's page on Facebook. Note the blue buttons, which you'll see anywhere you encounter these screens.

Here are the most common variations of the blue buttons:

- **Play Game:** For apps that are games (for example, Words with Friends or Candy Crush Saga), you click the Play Game button to begin playing right away.
- **Visit Website:** This button appears for apps that work primarily as an outside website that sends information back to Facebook. Clicking this button takes you to the website, where you're prompted to set up an account.

Figure 8-1: Want to use this app? Make sure you know what it's asking for.

- **Send to Mobile:** Many apps these days have a mobile integration as well as a Facebook integration. If you have a phone number linked to your account, you can click this button to send a link to your phone, where you can install the mobile app and link it to your Facebook account.
- **Go to App:** Some apps don't maintain separate websites. When you use these apps, you'll still feel like you're on Facebook, with the blue bar on top and the sidebar on the left. What you see in the center of the page, however, is dictated by the app developers, not by Facebook. Clicking the Go to App button starts your use of an app in Facebook.
- **Okay:** This button usually appears when you're already on another website and click to log in to Facebook. Clicking the Okay button gets you started on that website.

Although these buttons vary based on the kind of app and what it does, the same thing happens when you click any one of them: You agree to share your information with that app. That's why you need to pay attention to what the app is and what it's requesting before you agree.

Clicking *any* of these buttons has the same result: Your info will be shared with the app asking for it, and you'll be able to begin using that app.

In Figure 8-1, below the buttons and the list of information the app requires is a privacy drop-down menu (set on Public in this figure). This menu is familiar because you use it to select your privacy setting every time you post something to your Timeline. For apps, you can select a blanket setting just for posts from that app. In other words, even if I share all my posts publicly, I can choose to share my Candy Crush Saga posts just with friends. You'll find the following privacy options: Public, Friends of Friends, Friends, Friends Except Acquaintances, Only Me, or a custom set of people.

Sometimes, when I want to use an app but I don't want it posting back to Facebook on my behalf, I set the privacy to Only Me. For example, when I started using the Hulu app (Hulu is a website that streams television shows online), I decided I didn't need my friends knowing just how much I like teen dramas. I still wanted to use the app for creating a profile on Hulu and easily posting clips to Facebook. So I set the privacy to Only Me, which means I'm the only one who can see the automatically generated posts about my *Gossip Girl* marathon.

Now What? Using Apps on Facebook

Because so many different apps answer so many different needs, it's difficult to tell you what to do next. However, you will encounter some common prompts and onscreen actions. Read on to find out what form these might take.

Application Home pages on Facebook

When you click a Play Game or Go to App button, you'll likely be taken to the app's Home page. When you click a Visit Website button, you'll be taken to the app's website in a separate browser tab or window.

You can see a sample Home page (for Candy Crush Saga) in Figure 8-2. Its Home page basically prompts you to start playing the game. Notice that the blue bar is still at the top of the screen, which means that if you get bored playing this game, you can easily go back to your Facebook Home page or Timeline.

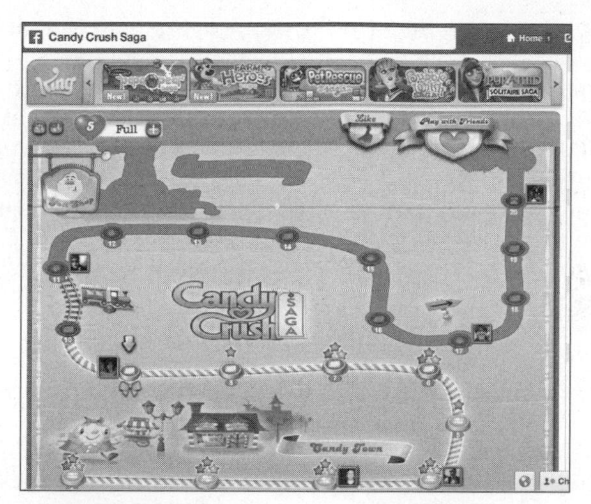

Figure 8-2: The Home page for Candy Crush Saga.

Sidebar links

The left sidebar on your Home page is where you go to get to different parts of Facebook: your groups, News Feed, events, and so on. Links to the apps you use most often will also appear in the sidebar, with the ones you use most often at the top. Click the See More link in the sidebar and scroll down to see all your apps and games.

If you've used lots of apps over time, you might not even see all of them when you click See More. After you expand the sidebar, scroll down to the Apps section and click the triangle icon next to the word Apps. The triangle should be pointed down when all your apps are displayed.

Invitations and requests

You can invite friends not only to events but also to play games or use apps with you. After your friends are playing the same game as you or using the same application, you can send them requests for specific actions. For example, many games enable you to send requests to people for specific items they may have accumulated through their own play.

The beauty of games on Facebook is that you can play against your friends, which means they can be opponents in word games, generals in your online armies, or tellers in your online banks. When you ask them to take part or send them something within the game, the game can send them a request on your behalf. Figure 8-3 shows the confirmation dialog box that you need to approve to send a request to a friend. That dialog box shows what the actual request will look like.

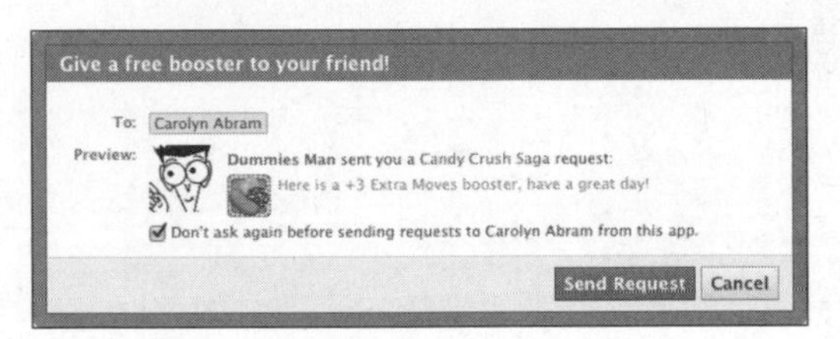

Figure 8-3: Sending requests.

In Figure 8-3, note the Don't Ask Again before Sending Requests to <*friend*>" check box below the preview. If you leave this check box selected, the app will be able to send that friend requests on your behalf as often as it wants. Clear this check box so that you always know when an app is sending your friend a request.

Posts

As you play games and use apps, you may also be prompted to post things to your Timeline. Figure 8-4 shows what one such prompt might look like. In this case, it's a game prompting you to share that you completed another level. If you want to share these achievements with friends, that's great; click the Share button and feel free to add your own comments to the text field.

If you'd rather not post to your Timeline about something like this, just click Cancel and continue on with whatever it was you were doing.

Figure 8-4: Posting to your Timeline (formerly known as the Wall).

Extra credit

Lots of games on Facebook allow you to purchase virtual goods within the game. For example, if you haven't yet gotten to the level needed to unlock an advantage in Candy Crush Saga, you could purchase that advantage (extra moves!) for a dollar or two. Some games create their own currency, which you buy, and some use Facebook Credits.

Facebook Credits is a payment system built by Facebook that other applications can incorporate into their service. Purchasing Facebook Credits is a way to purchase goods without sharing your credit card information with a million different game developers. Each credit costs ten cents, so one dollar gets you ten credits. Games may require different numbers of credits for different items.

Facebook Credits is just one of many payment systems you may come across while using apps.

Managing Your Apps

Depending on how you wind up using apps and how you feel about the ones you've added, a time may come when you want to change some things. To do so, go to your App Settings page by following these steps:

1. **Click the down arrow on the right side of the blue bar on top to access the Account menu.**

2. **Select Settings.**

   The Settings page appears. The different sections of this page are shown on the left side.

3. **Click Apps on the left side of the page.**

   The Apps tab of the Settings page appears.

On the Apps tab, you can see a list of all the apps you use, in order of which you've used most recently. Click Edit, located next to these apps, to see more information about how they work with Facebook. You can see the expanded information about an app in Figure 8-5. You can adjust the settings related to each app a number of ways, which I explain next.

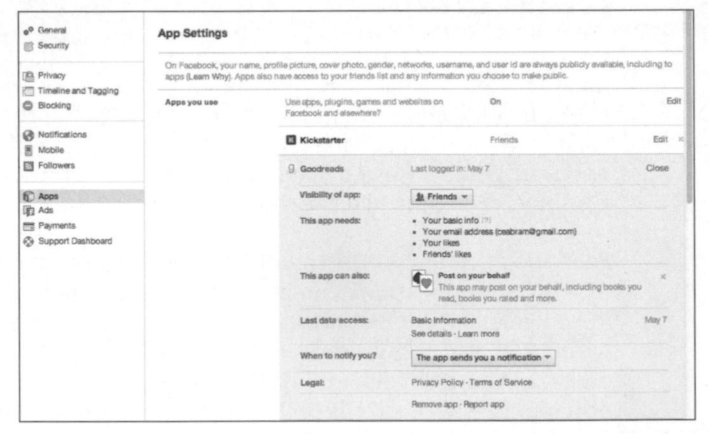

Figure 8-5: Check out the apps you use and how they use your info.

Removing apps

The simplest way to adjust how an app interacts with your information is simply to revoke its capability to interact with your information. This option makes sense only if you are 100 percent done with an app — that is, you don't plan to use it again in the future.

To remove an app, click the X next to its name in the list of your apps. A window pops up explaining that doing so removes it from your Facebook account, but that the app may still have some of the data you shared with it (it just won't get any new data going forward). You can then choose to delete all the app's activity on Facebook by selecting the Delete All Your *<app>* Activity on Facebook check box. Clicking the Remove button finishes the process.

When you remove an app, you will no longer be able to use the app, and it won't be able to send any information or posts to your Timeline or invitations to your friends. At the same time, because so many apps exist outside Facebook, you have to keep in mind that it will still be able to contact you via your e-mail address, and it may still have an account for you created via Facebook. If you want to cut off an app completely, you may have to delete your information and close your account on another website entirely.

Changing who can see an app's posts on your Timeline

If you're concerned about who can see the content an app is posting to your Timeline, you can always change the visibility of that app (and its posts) so fewer people can see it. To do so, follow these steps:

1. **Click Edit next to the app's name in the Apps You Use section of the App Settings page.**

   You see details about the ways this app can interact with your information and Timeline.

2. **Click the Privacy drop-down menu.**

   The menu is next to the Visibility of App section.

3. **Select who can see posts from this app.**

   You'll find the following privacy options: Public, Friends of Friends, Friends, Friends Except Acquaintances, Only Me, or a custom set of people. Selecting Only Me is a quick way to make sure that no one will see posts that the app creates on your behalf.

Preventing an app from posting and accessing info

As an alternative (or in addition) to changing who can see posts an app makes, you can revoke an app's capability to post to your Timeline altogether.

1. **Click Edit next to the app's name in the Apps You Use section of the App Settings page.**

   You see details about the ways this app can interact with your information and Timeline.

2. **Look in the This App Needs and the This App Can Also sections to see what permissions the app has.**

   Every app will list here that it can access your basic information and send you e-mail (Instant personalization apps such as Pandora or Yelp do not list your e-mail here). Depending on the app, it will also list any other Timeline info it requires and whether it can post on your behalf or access your information when you're not using the app.

3. **Click the X next to Post on Your Behalf, or Access Your Data Any Time, or both to revoke these permissions.**

   If you revoke the Post on Your Behalf setting, the app will no longer be able to make posts on your Timeline. If you revoke the Access Your Data setting, the app will no longer be able to access your data when you are not using it.

Changing notification settings

Apps may contact you via the Notifications section of your Home page. If you're being bothered by too many notifications, you can turn off this capability from the App Settings page.

1. **Click Edit next to the app's name in the Apps You Use section of the App Settings page.**

   You see details about the ways this app can interact with your information and Timeline.

2. **Use the drop-down menu in the When to Notify You section to select Never.**

If you previously turned off notifications and want to turn them back on, select The App Sends You a Notification.

Other app privacy settings

In addition to the Apps You Use section of the App Settings page, two other sections control how apps interact with your information.

- **Apps Others Use:** When your friends use other websites and apps with Facebook, they may find it useful to see their friends' (in this case, your) information — for example, a birthday calendar application, which may alert them when a friend's birthday is on the horizon. In this section, you can determine the information about you that your friends can allow sites to access. If you want your friends to be able to use a birthday reminder website to remember your birthday, you may want to allow them to give your birthday to the sites they trust. If you want to deny an application's access to some of your information, such as your education and work history, deselect the check box next to Education and Work History. Your friends won't be able to import that information into their apps.
- **Instant Personalization:** Instant Personalization is a way of instantly linking your Facebook account to partner sites. If you don't want Facebook doing this on your behalf, you can opt out here.

Controlling what you see from friends

News Feed can be a great way to discover what apps your friends use, but it also can be overrun with app stories, blocking out the interesting content that's not related to those games and apps. Here are a few tips to keep your News Feed (and the rest of your Facebook) from being cluttered by apps:

- **Hide from News Feed.** If your News Feed is inundated with posts from apps, click the small gray arrow that appears when you hover your cursor over that post.

A menu of options appears, including Hide. When you click Hide, the post disappears from News Feed and is replaced by text confirming that it has been hidden. Click the black Hide All Stories from *<app>* text to hide all future posts from that app.

- **Block an app.** If you find an app offensive or it keeps sending you invites or requests, you can block it. From the Settings page, navigate to the Blocking tab using the left menu and enter the app's name in the text field in the Block Apps section. The app will no longer be able to contact you via Facebook or see any of your info.
- **Block a friend's invites.** Sometimes just one person is the problem. The person may be sending you invites or requests from multiple apps, and it's driving you nuts. Navigate to the Blocking section of the Settings page, and enter your aunt's name in the text field in the Block App Invites section. Then, any invites or requests she sends you will automatically be ignored and won't generate any notifications on your Home page or in your e-mail. You'll still be friends with her, and you'll still see posts from her such as status updates and photos; you just won't get the app stuff anymore.

Opting out

If you're getting more and more queasy about the idea of using games and apps, you can consider opting out of using apps entirely. This isn't a step I recommend because applications can be a lot of fun and useful. But if you're very protective of your information, you can effectively turn off apps.

From the App Settings page, look at the top of the Apps You Use section. The first line item is not an app but a setting labeled Use Apps, Plugins, Games, and Websites on Facebook and Elsewhere?" Next to this question is the default setting of On. Click the Edit link to the right of this item to expand more information and a Turn Off Platform button.

Clicking this button effectively removes all the apps you have used and prevents your account information from being used by any application ever again.

Later, if you find an app you do want to use and you click any of the App Install Screen buttons, this setting will automatically turn back on.

Chapter 9

Ten Tips for Parents of Teens on Facebook

In This Chapter

- Talking to them about Internet safety
- Teaching them how to report abuse and block people
- Using Privacy settings

It's hard to put the word *teenager* together with the phrase *social networking* and not get just the teensiest bit anxious. A lot of horror stories are out there about cyberbullying and online predators. Any parent is likely to be a bit worried. However, it's unreasonable to think you can keep your teen away from Facebook, much less the Internet. That's where their friends are and that's where they want to be. So here are some tips I hope will be useful in navigating the waters of Facebook and the Internet at large.

Talk about Internet Safety

Here are some general Internet safety tips that apply no matter what kind of website you're using:

- Don't share any personal identifying info (address, phone number, credit card info, and so on) with anyone you don't know.
- Create different passwords for all the sites you use. Passwords should be difficult to guess and contain a mix of numbers, letters, and symbols.

- Don't share your passwords with anyone, even boyfriends, girlfriends, or best friends. (This is one that teenagers tend to struggle with.)
- Click only those links you trust; be wary of scammy-sounding advertisements. They are usually scams.

Beware of Strangers

On Facebook, in general, people are who they say they are and tend to have only one account that links to their real e-mail address and contains only real information about them. Unfortunately, like the real world, Facebook isn't free of malicious people who lie to take advantage of someone else.

The good news is that keeping your experience free of people like this is fairly easy if you accept Friend Requests only from people you know in real life. Talk to your teens about the importance of sharing information only with people they know and telling you when someone they don't know contacts them.

Report Abuse

Virtually every piece of content on Facebook — including photos, videos, messages, Timelines, groups, posts, and events — has a Report link. If your child comes across content that is abusive or offensive, report it by clicking any of the Report links located near these pieces of content. Facebook investigates all abuse reports and removes content that violates its Statement of Rights and Responsibilities. You can report Timelines for being fake or posts for being harassing.

Block People

Certain kinds of behaviors can lead to someone being kicked off of Facebook, but you (and your teen) might not want to wait around until the offender is out for good. If someone is bothering your teen and won't leave him or her alone, block the person from the Privacy Shortcuts menu. Blocking someone makes it seem like that person isn't on Facebook. Neither of you will be able to see each other in searches, to message each other, or to look at each other's Timeline.

To block someone, follow these steps:

1. **Hover the cursor over the left sidebar to expand it.**
2. **Click the lock icon next to your name at the top of the menu to open the Privacy Shortcuts menu.**
3. **In the Privacy Shortcuts menu, click the How Do I Stop Someone from Bothering Me section.**
4. **Type a name or an e-mail address in the Add Name or Email text box.**
5. **Click Block to add the person to your blocklist.**

Use Privacy Settings

Teens in the United States on Facebook have specific privacy rules that are different from most users. Their Public posts are available only to friends of friends — not distributed to everyone. However, you can rest easier if you go through your teen's Privacy settings with her and agree on settings that allow her to share more safely. In general, sharing only with friends or, better yet, creating a list of close friends can quickly ensure that fewer people are seeing your child's information and that you both have a complete list of who those people are. For more on privacy issues, see Chapter 3.

Talk about Posts and Consequences

Once something is shared, such as a Facebook photo or post, it's hard to undo. Encourage your teens to think about how something might be seen and interpreted by people who aren't their closest friends. Would they want a college admissions officer to see that photo? Would they want their boss to read that post? Remind your teens to think before they post.

Remember the Golden Rule

Talk to your kids about behaviors that might affect others, whether known or unknown, such as creating hateful Facebook groups targeting a teacher or a peer, or going into a forum on the Internet and posting something inflammatory or offensive under the protection of anonymity (although, on the Internet, anonymity doesn't usually last).

The Golden Rule applies to your teens just as much in adolescence as when they were in kindergarten: Do unto others as you would have them do unto you. Would you want someone saying something bad about you online? How would you feel if you posted something personal, and people made fun of you? Part of being part of Facebook (and other online communities) is being a good citizen. That makes Facebook Nation a safe place for all.

Respect Their Boundaries

After you get your teen set up on Facebook and talk about all the general ideas for Internet and Facebook safety, you need to give him or her some space.

Some kids are comfortable interacting with their parents; others think it is the most embarrassing thing in the world. When you were a teen, did you like it when your parents listened in on your phone calls or read your diary? When you ask to be friends with your teenagers, they can feel like you're invading their space. You can talk to them about some of the things you see on Facebook, but commenting on their stuff and posting on their Timeline might get you unfriended.

Don't Send Friend Requests to Your Teen's Friends

If your teen's friends friend you, it's probably okay to accept those requests (though you may want to check with your teen first; see the preceding section). But it's generally considered weird and pushy for you to reach out to your teen's friends.

Create a Family Group

If you joined Facebook just to understand what's going on in your teen's life, that's great. But now, having read this book, I hope you can see that there's a lot Facebook can offer you and your friends, with or without your children present. Share photos. Coordinate events with your friends. Post statuses about what's going on with you.

To keep your social life separate from your teen's social life but still have interactions on Facebook, create a family group. You can add lots of family members, and everyone can share the sort of stuff family members like to know: holiday newsletter–type stuff. It creates a space where it's okay for you and your son or daughter to interact on Facebook.

Index

• A •

• B •

• C •

• G •

• H •

• I •

• J •

• L •

• R •

• S •

• T •

• U •

• V •

• W •